IF I HAD A HAMMER

IF I HAD A

HAMMER

BY *Connie Johnson*

"ON ONE END A HAMMER CAN BUILD . . .
. . . AND THE OTHER END TAKE DOWN"

IF I HAD A
HAMMER

By Connie Johnson

Charleston, SC
www.PalmettoPublishing.com

Paperback ISBN: 978-1-68515-562-9
eBook ISBN: 978-1-68515-587-2

ACKNOWLEDGMENTS

I would like to give a thank you to the Palmetto publisher! Also to Payprov Publishing for critiquing my book! I would also like to acknowledge all my siblings and their spouses, children, nieces, nephews, aunts, uncles, godchildren I helped raise, and grandchildren that played a part in my life and I hold dear to my heart; for this, I love you all.

A special thank you to my dear Uncle William, Uncle Felix, and Uncle Lloyd for always being there when I needed you all the most. Dr. Byron Williams, who always kept it 100 percent with our community without compromise. To Kim Lanham, who fought with me and stayed true to our community; Anna Chestnut, my sis, who always had my back; Mrs. Velma Lovelace whom I adore; Joyce Brayboy, for all your help with our community events; Mrs. Shaun Smith, for your vision and integrity; Jonathan and Gertrude Hevita, who were a blessing in our lives and to the many youths who crossed my path. You were as much a blessing to me as anyone could ever imagine.

I know there are so many more to name, but truly I thank all, including my enemies, for moving me toward my destination. As Christ was being whipped, spat on, persecuted, ridiculed, etcetera, he knew his enemies were moving him toward his destination. He kept his eyes on the cross. This is a constant reminder of what we all must do.

Features: Mrs. Shaun Smith; Byron Williams; the Hevitas; Dr. Goldstone; Coach Craig Davis, Kiana, Kadeija, Keyaira, and Konnie Johnson.

DEDICATION

I would like to dedicate my book to my Lord and Savior Jesus, Yeshua, the Christ, and The Most High, who is my covering; he guided my path and stayed true to me even when I turned my back on him!

Honor to my parents who raised me, Ida and the late Elmer Ingram (SIP)—I thank you so much for all the love you both have sown. To my wonderful stepdad, Hubert Lobban, who treated us like his own. I was truly surrounded by so much love, and for that, I love you. To my biological dad, Johnathan DuBose Sr., (SIP). Thank you for planting the seed that brought forth life. I am grateful!

TABLE OF CONTENTS

Chapter 1:
EARLY YEARS

Growing up in the streets of Bridgeport, Connecticut, for me in the seventies was such a pleasant experience. When we were little, young and full of life, we did not know the challenges our parents faced. All we knew was that we had all our needs met and we had each other. I would like to briefly walk you down my past to understand the future purpose, The Most High, had in store for me.

Bridgeport, Connecticut, home of Barnum & Bailey Circus, was once inhabited by the Paugussett Native American tribe, only to become a colony in 1644. As of 2015 Bridgeport, Connecticut, was ranked 88 out of 100 in a list of the most dangerous cities in America according to an article written by *The Patch*.

Born to Elmer Ingram and Ida, in 1970, I can remember safely playing outside day and night in what still stands as Beardsley Terrace on the North End of Bridgeport. I grew up in Buildings 2, 3, and 8. At least four of my aunts and my grandparents lived in Building 3. I remember there being so much peace in my grandmother's home, even when she watched so many of us at the same time. She provided a solid structure. You see, Grandmomma was a woman of God and great faith. Ella Mae McGill-Brown was the glue that held our family together. She provided the structure, as it should be. Pops ruled with an iron fist and set the foundation. Luther Barr-Eaddy Brown did not talk much, but all I knew is that I felt protected as he made provisions and he set a strong foundation for us all.

They had a strong home built with strong roots. No storm could tear down this holy matrimony.

For our grandparents' fiftieth anniversary, our family rented a hall, and every one of their twelve children, grandchildren, and great-grandchildren all came together in ministry to celebrate this joyous occasion. Relatives from South Carolina, Virginia, and Detroit joined in on these festivities. My mother was the director of the children's choir and had me lead a song entitled "If I Had a Hammer." Building requires a hammer. This will tie into my story later.

In the summer months, I can remember going to Newfield Park with R & B music playing, such as Marvin Gaye's "Got to Give it Up," James Brown's "Get Up," Al Green's "Let's Stay Together," The Staples Singers' "I'll Take You There," Stevie Wonder's "Superstition," and The O'Jays' "Family Reunion," just to name a few, and watching my fine-looking uncles and friends who were well shaped get out the car with their golden baseball uniforms representing our side of town. You see, there were no gangs in those days. Sports and family would be considered gangs at that time. I also remember my oldest sister taking me for walks to Beardsley Park and us swimming and diving into a bay-like area with other area neighborhood kids. I remember going to drill team practices with my best friend, Ruthie, whom I will never forget. Life was so good and full of peaceful and joyful memories at this time. There were also bad memories but the good outweighed the bad. Although we were poor, it didn't seem as if we were. The fact was that we knew the Lord kept us close and content.

The Dark Side of Bridgeport

Although family life was good in my memory, my sisters had it rough in Beardsley Projects. I can remember my older sister, who was a Vanessa Williams look-alike, always having to fight girls who came over our home to jump her. My other beautiful sister Lisa had to always figure out another path to get us home safe from Wilbur Cross Elementary School due to bullies wanting to fight her. As the baby sister, I feared for my sisters all the time. It appears my sisters had to defend themselves every day. This was the environment in the school district full of teachers that did not look like us.

Families were against families, and the family you chose to hook up with determined the power you had in our community. One day my beautiful middle sister, Lisa, had enough and faced her bully. When she did, she developed quite the reputation of being someone not to mess with. After that, my sister did not take any mess from anyone. My mother made it out of town before the crack epidemic took over our community. How is this relevant to what you were talking about previously?

Chapter 2:

ON THE MOVE

As I stated at the beginning, we as children were unaware of the challenges our parents had to face in the projects, so my mother and her boyfriend moved us to Detroit, Michigan, in 1976, which was the beginning of the disco era. Detroit was just as memorable as Bridgeport, Connecticut. A place full of culture and promises for our people, the home of Motown, "The Big Three" automotive makers, gospel artist legends such as James Cleveland, Aretha Franklin, and the very talented Clark Sisters. Downtown was so off the hook with festivals, live performances, Hudson fireworks, entertainment, and games that everyone dressed to kill. The environment had everyone full of ambition and admiration for the talents that came out of this vibrant city. The education system was full of teachers and principals that looked like us, and if we dared to step out of line, there would be a paddle on our rear end.

During the weekends my siblings and I would race to the TV to watch *Soul Train*, and Mondays through Fridays, I was mesmerized by the Detroit dance show *The Scene*, which imitated *Soul Train*. Detroit dances were like none other, as we would do dances like the Shake and Snake.

Every Sunday morning my mother had us in church choir. My mother became a leader wherever she planted her foot. She became the head of choir director at a particular Brookroad Baptist Church in Detroit, Michigan. My oldest sister's troubles continued in Detroit with females, not because of her beauty but because of her talent. Sister can sing! I continued to watch my sisters being targeted, which taught me how to fear no one.

Moving Too Much

Our first place in Detroit was on Pilgrim Street. My brother Timothy made a name for himself very quickly after winning the talent show at Central High School playing "I Wish" by Stevie Wonder, and again my older sister stood out with her looks. But we stayed there less than a year. From Pilgrim Street, my mother ran into a good sum of money but couldn't place the home in her name because she was on welfare. She placed the home in her brother's name. The street was Fleming Street. We were in a huge house where each of us had our own room; there was a huge basement with a kitchen where my mother would host parties for teenagers, charging fifty cents per person. She would also sell food from the kitchen for a huge profit. The parties made our family popular overnight. My oldest sister had a male friend who was the top DJ in the community that my mother used for the parties. I was looking at and learning how my mother operated, putting together functions while bringing a community together. Our parties were the talk of the town. And our family became the one family not to mess with on that side of Detroit. At first the Gallaghers were the top family, but that changed quickly. Together, we were a force to be reckoned with.

From Fleming, my mother uprooted us to move to a rough part of Detroit, Sorrento. Huge rats ran through our house, while others would be pregnant in our backyard.

This move began to affect me because I stuck my nose into a bullying situation in which I became a target. This is when I learned something about myself. I do not like injustice or seeing people being bullied. I noticed I stood up for the weak, which got me in trouble at this new school. The bully began to target me. I did not tell my mother because that was how we dealt with situations. But thank God, my mother moved again, to the North Side of Detroit, to Lothrop Street. My sister and brother ended up attending the same high school as The Temptations and The Supremes, Northwestern High School.

Things only got worse when we moved to Warren and Twenty-Fifth Street. This area was crime infested and the worst side of town in Detroit, as it is today. My family was miserable, but it was a short-lived stay; we soon got out before the crack epidemic hit the urban communities.

My mother then moved us to another state, Virginia, to the city of Richmond, with all my siblings but one. My oldest brother Timothy stayed in Michigan. This move saved my siblings' life. My brother Calvin made a quick name for himself as he was a basketball favorite at Highland Springs High School, and my sister Lisa who was now five months pregnant, made a name for herself after rising to the top of academics only to be chosen at this new school in the top ten of homecoming queens. My troubles began there in Virginia.

Chapter 3:

TROUBLED TEEN

A s my mother worked a job at Henrico Hospital in Virginia, and everyone was doing their thing, I ended up having idle time and was up to no good. There was a neighboring house in where the parents allowed anyone and everyone to skip school and hang out. This bred hell in the community. I began skipping school at this house, sleeping with multiple partners, fighting, and stealing. My mother and stepdad thought of me as this innocent, well-mannered, respectful little girl but had no idea the dark side that I had hidden so well. Now I often encourage parents to be mindful and vigilant concerning who their children are hanging around and keep them busy. In several instances, for example, females surrounded me to fight me. I would always grab the leader of the group and wear her out. These things prepared me for what was to come.

Had I taken advantage of what Richmond had to offer, I would have been an outstanding leader in a positive way, but negative influences led me to choose negative people to hang around, which caused a negative environment around me. One negative influencer in my life was my mother's husband. He and his partner would have a tiny lady go in and come back out as if she were pregnant. She was carrying stolen clothes inside her coat, would come to the car and take them all out before my eyes. They would sell these outfits to the community. I then began to dream of going to the same mall and doing the same thing. I called it STD (spiritually transferred disease). At my first attempt, I was caught immediately. God chastises those he loves because he has a greater purpose for us. I became a menace in Richmond, but I loved the very ground it was on. Richmond had so much to offer to the youth. I wish I had taken advantage of it as soon as I stepped foot on it.

There were many different after-school activities, but I chose to hang out with other misguided teens. I developed such a bad reputation, and I asked the Lord to get me out. And so he did!

Back to Connecticut

In 1985 the hip-hop culture took over! The song "Roxanne, Roxanne" by UTFO was the number-one song on the chart. An answer back by Roxanne Shontae had the youth going berserk! Fur coats and bamboo earrings were the thing the first year at Central High School, Bridgeport, Connecticut. I was around all my family but never again felt so alone. I was the last child to be home and eager to be back around my family. What I expected to happen did not happen. Everyone moved up and out of the projects, owned homes, and was working middle-class jobs. The family mindset had changed. Friends became our family more so than our family. My vision when I moved back to Connecticut was how we used to be in the Terrace. I do understand we must grow and move up, but many of our people do not know how to handle the elevation. Instead of remaining humble, we become judgmental of individual lifestyles and grandstands. We think we have arrived in the "deluxe apartment in the sky" but it is crumbs given to us to keep us content and in our place. In fact, this was to prevent another Nate Turner from rising. Staying true to who we are and admitting who we are must open the reality for us to begin to dig deeper for our deliverer and redeemer. This is how we stay connected to the Most High and not this fake, false sense of success stemming from money, power, control, and fame. All these urges can lead to abuse of alcohol, drugs, and sex abuse, which play a huge part in our families separating and divorcing. Divorces always separate families, which ultimately separates communities, I attest to this. 1 John 2:15-17 King James Version15 Love not the world, neither the things that are in the world. If any man love the world, the love of the Father is not in him.16 For all that is in the world, the lust of the flesh, and the lust of the eyes, and the pride of life, is not of the Father, but is of the world. **17** And the world passeth away, and the lust thereof: but he that doeth the will of God abideth for ever.

Things could not be the same. Our cousins, who had both parents' outlook on life, differed from the divorced parents' children. Again, I found myself on my own, even though my entire family was around. What the enemy tried to use for bad in Richmond, the Most High placed upon my heart to make building up a community my strength.

You remember early on in chapter 1 when I spoke about my singing a song, "If I had a Hammer?" This song was a prophecy in which God revealed my given purpose, which was to build a community. The song goes like this:

> If I had a hammer, I'd hammer in the morning!
> I'd hammer in the evening! All over this land!
> I'd hammer out of danger!
> I'd hammer out of warning!
> I'd hammer the love between my brothers and my sisters
> All over this Land!

What a powerful and fitting song for my story!

Chapter 4:

BUILD

My parents moved again from the North End to the East End on Central Avenue in Bridgeport, Connecticut, where I attended Warren Harding High School (WHHS) during the 1985–1986 school year. There I played basketball, chorus and theater. I quickly became known for my talents and my no-nonsense personality. Yes, I was known by many but hung out with no one at the time. That was how I was. This one day I was approached in the gym by several girls talking, he said, she said. As I focused on the leader and what I would do to her, she quickly pushed my head. And there it was—the leader of the pack and I were tussling. The gym teachers tackled me, pinning me to the ground. As I reminisce and look back on my childhood, my purpose was set in stone. My fight would always be against leaders. As it turned out, the rest of the girls surrounded me and focused on the leader; who could have known this would be a part of my testament in the future, my no-nonsense approach and focus on corrupt leadership? That was not the case in this situation because my God approach was a shadow of what God had purposed for my life.

My mother was more vehemently on a mission than the apostles in the New Testament. She would go from town to town without any fear or worries. I then went to Detroit for one year and landed back at WHHS, where I graduated in 1988. I visited the office of the principal,

Dr. Goldstone, to ask permission to start a drill team. Dr. Goldstone was 100 percent supportive of my plan. I asked others about my plan and if they would like to join. I even asked my soon-to-be best friend, Cherise, if she would like to join, but she did not answer me at that time.

On November 23, 1987, the day before the annual Thanksgiving game, the Pep Assembly took place in the boys' gym. The assembly went smoothly and much school spirit was shown by every class, especially the Seniors. The Flag Squad, the band, and the Color Guard performed sensationally. The Drill Team was the highlight of the assembly. With excitement in the air, students enjoyed themselves tremendously. To add more to the fun the D.J. "White Flash" performed after the assembly.

What's the next move? Tawanna Parrish

Robert Simmons, John Ramsey, Ricardo Liera with the beat.

"We ain't no joke!"

The Pep Rally

Our dance team's first performance took place the day before the biggest rivalry games in any urban community in Connecticut, Central High School versus WHHS—the Thanksgiving Day Game! But first, the band began to play, then the drum line stood up and led the way down the path on the gym floor. After that, the newest and only drill team in Bridgeport, Connecticut, came stepping with such confidence right behind the drum line. There were only a few of us, dressed in a WHHS blue hoodie and sweatpants that read WHHS Presidents with our names on the back. The crowd went wild! A sense of pride resonated in the atmosphere. We again performed at the Thanksgiving Day Game, which was the very next day. This drew more spectators. That we had a drill team drew attention to the other area high schools, and people were eager to see what folks were talking about. The WHHS Step Team went out with such boldness behind the drum line. This developed even more school spirit at WHHS, bringing more unity and togetherness.

Central versus WHHS Basketball '87

Central High School had been preparing its girls to dance at halftime at this highly anticipated game in Connecticut. These games are so intense because these two rival schools despised each other. The Harding Girls came out drilling, which became old. Central busted out with an intense performance with twenty girls that put WHHS to shame. Yes, it was embarrassing, but this setback was a setup for our comeback!

Over forty girls from WHHS showed up to try out because we could not sleep on Central High School the next time later in the season. My girl Cherise Broadnax ended up joining our former step team; we had by then become a dance team. Cherise Broadnax was the baddest dancer in the town of Bridgeport. No one could top her skills. Michael and Janet Jackson, *what!* She rocked and served you hip-hop dances. When she stepped out on the floor, the crowd always went wild! I taught Cherise the dances from Detroit, and after she learned the dances, she took them to another level. She was dope! Nonetheless, we had a moral code—do not cut any dancers. If there were any dancers slow at learning, Cherise or the other two captains would take turns working with them until they got it. Every day, five days a week, two hours a day after school, we worked up a sweet performance until it was perfected. We put our money together to buy outfits in our school colors. The team of thirty-six girls wore royal blue, while the captains stood in front wearing yellow.

The day had come for us to bring *showtime* during halftime. The bleachers were packed! Cherise did her Janet Jackson move in the middle of the basketball court, and we were not to move until she pointed back at us. We stood still in a militant position. The crowd was going crazy at Cherise's performance! She pointed at us, and then we began to march! Stump, stump, stump, stump, stump, with opposite arms folded behind our backs at each step until we went to our spot in the middle of the court. Heavy D and The Boys began to play, and the captains began to dance with the James Brown dance first. OMG—it was so intense and wild! The dancers began to back us up. There was twirling in the air, back bending with hip hop moves to perfection. After we rocked the performance, we marched off the floor. Meanwhile, as we took our position along the sidelines, we were stretched out from one end of the court to another. A helper came behind us to pass out papers in our hands, like a relay runner passing the baton.

WHHS Gospel Choir

Central High School Got Smoked!

Central High School had on troop jackets. There were many of them. You see, Central High School was in the bougie section of Bridgeport so their parents could afford those expensive jackets owned by Jewish brothers and a Korean man that targeted our community with their sale. The cost was easily $180 or more. They took off their jackets on the sideline opposite us and walked out to the middle of the floor. Right before their routine, all our girls assumed our position and began to read the newspaper, causing a huge distraction. Some girls were doing splits while reading the paper between their legs; I had a dancer on me and another girl's back as we bent over touching butt to butt. She had her legs crossed while sitting on our backs while reading her paper. Others stood beside the crowd with the open paper saying to them the chant "Extra, extra, read all about it." The Central High School girls became utterly distracted and began to mess up their routine. They left the floor disgusted and embarrassed.

We were youth just having fun, but the point I would like to address is that while crack began to invade the communities in the eighties, the Most High had purposed me to get together a few girls that could have been swept away in this pandemic or even become pregnant, to keep these beautiful individuals' minds focused and bodies busy to the point they had no time to partake in negativity. It grew to the point that girls from Central, Bassick, and Bullard Haven started back up their dance team. Each school brought so much school spirit and love to the environment. This was a credit to Dr. Goldstone and our teacher Mrs. Young, who was our adviser. So, in essence, had I been involved with my school family at Warren Harding High School, I would not have been led to step out of my comfort zone to open the doors for many.

The Most High knows what doors to close to find the open door.

"I'd hammer the love between my brothers and my sisters all over this land!"

After graduation, My family and I (Baby Girl and Soon to be Husband) got out of Bridgeport, Connecticut just in time before the crack epidemic was in full effect. This was a great move to save the father of my firstborn, I have no doubt he would have been a statistic.

For this to happen, they had to get rid of those who were positively affecting the community. Dr. Goldstone was the guy whom they had to let go. After this occurrence, the community went downhill.

Although the crack epidemic hit urban communities throughout the United States, Bridgeport was mainly affected due to everyone being packed into projects to kill each other. Unlike Detroit where the entire city was filled with so-called African Americans, Bridgeport didn't stand a chance and was ranked #1 in murders. In 1993, The police department had a videotape showing a half dozen young men, barely out of their teens, dressed in black ninja outfits and carrying semi automatic assault rifles. They took over my once beautiful city. (Ref: Edmind Mahony A Corner where Crack Is King*Nov.1992) That year, there were 168 Homicides reported in and around the City's East Side.

Chapter 5

RAISING THE DEAD

After graduation, in my late teens, I had my first child. My childhood demons revisited me. Of course, I got caught immediately. The Most High has his way of keeping us on track. My future husband packed our things in a U-Haul with the money we had saved, and we moved to Michigan where we both had family. In fact, his mother and father were raised in Michigan. His mother attended the same high school in Michigan I attended for a year in 1984, Pershing High School. So, it wasn't a hard decision.

My husband and I married and had our second child in 1994. Soon after, we had another child in 1996. Detroit is not the place where marriages can survive. There were so many beautiful-looking men and women and so many to choose from. You would have to move out of Detroit for marriages to survive unless you were raised with high morals, values, and standards and took them with you wherever you went. But when you are young, hard-headed, misguided, and surrounded by others who don't know Christ, you can easily be led astray.

In 1999 I became so burdened that I went to the doctor to get a prescription for my stress and depression. When I took the pills, they made me feel so high and disoriented that I was worse off than before. I cried out to the Lord for material things the entire time in Michigan, but God would never answer my prayers. I began to ask the Lord for wisdom and knowledge, and he began to open my eyes.

I was led to attend a church service in which there was an altar call. I was not too proud to ask for help. My soul was dead. A walking dead person, that is! As the lady walked me to the back, I began to weep. The lady began to minister to me, and she then asked me to talk to our Father. I started off not knowing what to say. She then told me to talk to him like I would talk to my friend. It was not going anywhere. She then told me to share how I felt or even let him have it. I began to tell off my Father—not that he had to do with my situation, but I spilled out my heart. Several minutes later I began to cry uncontrollably, and at that moment, when I released what was in my heart, it allowed the Holy Spirit to be poured into my heart. It felt like I was on cloud nine. A rebirth had taken place. All my heavenly burdens were lifted at that moment. The Most High sent a comforter to do just that. Mathew 11-28 KJV *Come unto me, all ye that labour and are heavy laden, and I will give you rest.* Also, I was encouraged by 2 Corinthians 5:17, which states that when you are in Christ, *you are a new creator, old things are passed away, behold all things are new.* I felt Jesus's presence in me from that day forward. What used to bother me, no longer did. I began to call everyone whom I felt I had wronged to repent to them. You see, I have always believed in the Lord, but when we are young, we think we have time to sin, but I am here to tell you, we are in the last days. Time is of the essence.

For nine months, the entire time I was pregnant with my fourth child, I studied the Book of Proverbs and the mind of Christ.

  began to hear his voice each day directing my path. Things got harder and harder, the opposite of getting better. He opened my eyes to this world and the world to come.

Psalms 34:19: "Many are the afflictions of the righteous: but the Lord delivered him out of them all."

Chapter 6

MY GIFTS MADE MANIFEST

The first time I realized that The Most High's gifts had manifested in me of prophecy, new tongue and interpretation of tongues was when I began to clearly understand the Word of God through the Holy Spirit, understand the testimony of The Apostles, who is the foundation of the Body of Christ and understood Paul the apostle, Epistles. The light switch came on in my head almost immediately just like the day of Pentecost in the upper room. An utterance of mysteries in the spirit. It is not by might, not by power, but by His spirit (paraphrasing Zechariah 4:6).

Before the Holy Spirit came upon me, reading the bible was extremely hard to comprehend. Many people believe speaking in tongues (new language) is this weird utterance in the flesh of sounds or babbling (like Televangelist, Paula White or Pastor Creflo Dollar), most have seen on T.V. and religious movies. Meanwhile, most false teachers do not know what they are saying, never interpret their utterance or enchantment. Acts like this run people away from church which was why Christ states in1 Corinthians 14:5, *I would that ye all spake with tongues, but rather that ye prophesied: for greater is he that prophesieth than he that speaketh with tongues, except he interpret, that the church may receive edifying.* When someone speaks to a stranger or The Body of Christ, inspired by The Most High, typically a warning or edification, and it comes to pass, the body of Christ will be strengthen which makes prophesying as powerful than speaking in a new language (knowledge of The Most High through the Holy Spirit building up Christ). These are The Chosen Ones which are few.

When I was working at my first job after moving back to Bridgeport. I was working inside this place in Fairfield, Connecticut, that had several different offices and a karate class inside this one building, and this lady knew that I worked there, and we pulled up at the same time to park. I was driving this old, beat-up company vehicle from around 1978. It looked like the Brady Bunch station wagon. As I was pulling back to get in my parking space, she began getting out of the car. In her anger, I could tell she was highly prejudiced in her conversation as she began to accuse me of getting too close to her vehicle and bumping her vehicle. This was far from the truth. As she argued with me, I was assisting my mildly retarded clients, attempting to transition them into the building. She followed me and knew exactly where I worked, went to my boss, and began sharing her side of the story about how I had bumped her vehicle. By all evidence presented, they could tell she was lying.

My First Prophecy
As she began to walk out, I looked at the young lady, and I spoke to her about how wrong she was. I was unhappy that she had falsely accused me, and I prophesied that her punishment was going to be three times as great as the lie she had spread about me. Exactly three weeks later, I heard some people talking in the hallway among other karate moms. They were gathered around this very same lady who had accused me wrongly of hitting her vehicle and were asking what happened to her vehicle because it was badly damaged. At the time I didn't know but heard her describing her hitting a deer in an accident. I don't know where she was coming from or going to, but she had hit a deer, and she explained to them that the adjuster had stated that there was over $3,000 worth of damages. At that moment I reflected on what I said, and again this was like three weeks from the time she had falsely accused me. It was three times the damage of the car she claimed I damaged, which was the prophecy I had shared

with her. To me, it wasn't a big prophecy, but that was the Lord letting me know that I had the power of the Holy Spirit dwelling in me, and he reminded me that my words would be powerful. God would be using me to not only build but to also reproof, and that's powerful.

God began using me in a mighty way. When you remain humble and walk in the fear of the Most High, this fear is a healthy fear; it's pleasing to him that you revere him. He will move mountains for you; he will manifest his presence in you and his gifts in you. As a result, he began to enlarge my territory. Soon thereafter, I began coaching and using my director's skills for the WHHS Gospel Choir. I was heavily involved in my daughter's life. While I was coaching, as an assistant coach, the girls JV team from Warren Harding, was excelling and punishing teams. Our school had not won or even advanced to state in years. They barely won one out of three games per season, even while I was on the team in 1986. WHHS's team always struggled.

My daughter had played basketball from the time she was ten, and by the time she had gotten to high school, she had made a name for herself in the community. She and others on her team were a force to be reckoned with. Her teammate Bug was a power forward who dominated the post, while my daughter played the center position. My daughter was trained skillfully in Michigan and brought forth her talent to my home city and school. She went on to go to the University of Connecticut (UConn) basketball camp and won the championship. She appeared in an article in The Connecticut Post, being listed as the Most Valuable Player at this summer camp. Later she joined forces with my alma mater, a warm-hearted high school, and I began coaching there as well. I had coached in Michigan at AAU and with that experience, brought my experience to my school, WHHS. Together with the other coach there, I started off really well. Our girls had a nearly undefeated season, only losing two games that year. This meant that these girls who were junior varsity in a freshman class were the ones that we needed to watch out for the next couple years. In one game, the JV girls we were playing were from the toughest team in Connecticut. This was the dominant Fairfield Warde Team Both coaches were respected throughout the entire state of Connecticut. They received multiple end-of-game recognitions and championships, and his program throughout the years supported my JV girls. Even as we played his JV girls, we succeeded to the point where the head coach of Fairfield got up and started trying to help the opposing JV coach beat this Warren Harding team. We prevailed! You would think that because of our triumph over this giant of a man, the head coach would appreciate and be proud of all of us. However, he began being envious. Our girls ended up with a wonderful, wonderful season. They were just shy of the states, but just imagine if we had stuck together for another couple of years—we would have been champions. That same coach created strife to get rid of me and could not rest while I was in my position. Shortly afterward I moved my coaching gifts and talents over to Kolbe Cathedral High School. My gift of wisdom and the skills of how to coach were given to me by the Almighty. I was walking in my anointment. I did everything to please my Father in heaven.

Kolbe was a well-established school and team that had a wonderful existing coaching staff. Coach Patton from Saint Joseph's High School and I had joined the coaching staff at Kolbe Cathedral. It was like a match made in heaven. We had different qualities and different skills, but with our coming together, we successfully brought forth an undefeated season of nineteen wins. These groups of young ladies each had amazing talent and out-of-this-world work ethics that paid off in the end.

Second Prophecy—Scrimmage Set For WHHS

The coach from my old school, WHHS, who had me removed, reached out to Kolbe's head coach Hodge and on this day wanted to set up a scrimmage. We met with the head coach from Kolbe to set up that date. We ended up going to play against the school I had just left. On the morning of the scrimmage, the coach from Harding contacted the coach from Kolbe Cathedral, and my second prophecy was given as a result. He contacted Coach Hodge claiming that he wasn't feeling well and that he was going to reschedule this scrimmage. By knowing him and his ways, I knew that he had something up his sleeve, so I spoke to the head coach at Kolbe and warned him that he needed to move forward with the game because the other coach would make it appear that they had forfeited. I could see that he was going to have his girls ready in a locker room, encouraging them on. I explained that I knew how he operated. As a result, the head coach from Kolbe Cathedral and I got in our car and drove over to Warren Harding High School, where we sure enough saw the head coach in the bleachers with the referees. They had the time clock set and had security waiting there. As we walked into the room where the girls were all suited up, ready to play, gathering around him, as he was giving them a pep talk. The head coach from Kolbe approached him, reminded him of the false claim that the scrimmage would be canceled or rescheduled, and told him that he had to give us fifteen minutes to prepare. We drove over to pick up the girls, came back to Warren Harding, played the game, and beat this team. I hate to say it, but even though it was my alma mater, there was an evil force in this school that needed to be exposed. Coach Hodge put the hammer on this team and defeated them by over seventy points. Now the head coach from Kolbe Cathedral and the JV coach had a great season. We went on to go 19–0 in the state and won the league championship. My freshman girls had suffered only two losses. It was such a wonderful season. This meant they were the team to beat if they stayed together for the next couple of years. The varsity girls also won the league championship as well as the state champion that year. I went on to coach another year with Kolbe Cathedral, and we fell short in both the league and the state tournament. My time was up, not because of the loss but because I started sensing the same thing I had felt with the WHHS coaching staff. One must know when to listen to the still voice of the Lord. Plant the seed and allow others to water it. On to my next assignment in using the hammer (building).

The race is not given to the swift or to the strong but to the one who endures to the end. Ecclesiastes 9:11 KJV

Chapter 7

FIGHTING WITCHES AND WARLOCKS

It takes a village to raise a child...the right kind of village, that is!

Ephesians 6:12 (KJV): "For we wrestle not against flesh and blood, but against principalities, against powers, against the rulers of the darkness of this world, against spiritual wickedness in high places."

My second youngest daughter, Keyaira, was an ambitious, free-spirited, full of life child who was also brutally honest. This is something that was inherited and no fault of her own.

While we were in Michigan, the teachers and folks there allowed her to be herself as she blossomed. The moment we moved to Bridgeport, Connecticut, the controlling, manipulative spirits did not do well with Keyaira and the rest of her family. You see, God would use her boldness in a mighty way when she became seasoned. The enemy knew that and tried breaking her down from day one in Connecticut.

Because she had a lot of energy, the principal recommended she be placed in special education. I refused to allow the schools to place a label on any of my daughters because they no longer had the patience required by a real teacher. Once I took a stance, that was the beginning of her being targeted. My daughter had a bright young teacher who tried to protect her, but because the head was evil, there was not but so much she could do. I would find my daughter becoming a part of her environment. It takes a village to raise a child...the right kind of village, that is! Keyaira was becoming increasingly aggressive and angry.

One day I had to bring her lunch to the school, and once I left, I noticed some teachers surrounding this young child who was crying at the end of the slide. I thought another child had hurt herself but came to find out it was my daughter being bullied by these teachers. I received a phone call from the school's principal requesting that I come back to the school because there had been an incident. Once I arrived, I was told my daughter was having a bad day and needed to go home. The principal never informed me what the teachers had done. Some parents would not believe their children over other adult parents, so it was good that I saw what I saw. My daughter explained that because she had gone down the slides before another student who looked like them, they chose to bully her. She said it was her at the bottom of the slide. My heart dropped. I was so angry that I had witnessed what I thought was help being offered to a student but in fact was them bullying my own child. I vowed to fight back. As a result, the principal resigned, and years later, while my daughter worked for Yale, she saw one of the teachers that bullied her in the emergency room looking extremely old and decrepit. My daughter approached her, asking if she remembered her, and she fled the hospital in panic mode.

Another situation that formed the shape of my daughter at the hands of an unhealthy community was a vicious rumor started by a family member raising doubt about her being my husband's child, about which I later learned. This lie caused great harm to her with this new village way of life. Mental and physical abuse became the norm at the hands of family members, causing her to accept abuse in her later years and to have physical aggression for being rejected.

> *Proverbs 16:28 KJV: "A froward man soweth strife: and a whisperer separateth chief friends."*

When adults abuse their authority, children are raised to have no respect for the very same people who are supposed to lead and guide them on a healthy path. This was not a healthy community to raise children in. The children were being taught to bully by the adults. We become a product of our environment.

The hammer can be used to build, and it can be used to take down too!

> *Galatians 6:7 (KJV): "Be not deceived; God is not mocked: for whatsoever a man soweth, that shall he also reap."*

Segregation in the Stratford School District

My daughter Kadeija was at one time very quiet but observant. Once we moved here to Connecticut, one of the teachers tried changing her name from Kadeija to Kady. This can also change a person's identity. I don't believe she meant any harm, but the enemy knows, once you change our name, you change our identity.

My mother-in-law questioned why she was doing this and warned me to not allow this to happen. I took heed of what she said and spoke with the teacher. I noticed Kadeija began hanging around kids that were not within her culture and took more to the Spanish culture after a while. The Spanish culture treated Kadeija with so much love and respect. She was the teacher's pet at every school she attended. She had great teachers at Franklin Elementary School who prepared her for middle school. She scored higher than the district on her CMT in math and was at the district's reading level, which was good. Stratford was one of the highest-ranked district schools at the time. Once she arrived at middle school, my daughter's behavior began to change. She was not that happy little girl she had once been.

One day I received a phone call from the principal stating she had Kadeija in the office because the kids inside her class were bullying her. The principal commended me for raising a strong little girl who kept her peace amid what was happening. The young boys often protected Kadeija from the young girls in her class but could not protect her from the pain inside. She would never inform me what was going on because she knew how I got down. Momma didn't play that and would be right at the school handling my business which sometimes was unfortunate because she was left alone to cope with things by herself. Once I started to ask my daughter more questions, she revealed to me that she was inside the classroom with exclusively black and some Hispanic kids who happened to be from the projects in Stratford. Things were OK with me until she stated this fact about the class being all blacks and Hispanics. I then asked her where all the Caucasian students were. She stated they were on the Pie team. I asked her which team she was on, she stated she was on Infinity. I began to think about what was going on but needed more proof. Then came report card night. I could hear parents questioning other parents as to which team their child was in. One would brag about a child being in the Pie team. All were Caucasian. I heard this multiple times that night. I began to seek more answers and found out that Infinity was not being taught the same academics as Pie, whose academics were at a higher level. I proceeded to ask the principal why my daughter had been placed in the Pie group even when she had scored high on her CMT. She could not explain. By then it was too late. That environment took a toll on her. Some of the students sought to break her down mentally and socially. It may have worked for a little while, but it made her a stronger person in handling our culture.

As a result, I wrote a letter to the superintendent demanding that our children be given equitable treatment and that segregation in this district cease. Superintendent Robinson agreed and made the necessary changes, although I do hear that some black students fight to get into the AP and honors classes with their peers; some are granted the same opportunities as others.

Relational Aggression

My God was blessing me and my entire household from 2005-2007. My eldest daughter, Koniesha, had a great level of influence in the community, where she had favor with prominent people. At the time not only was she a scholar and bright, but she was also gentle, kind, loving and caring. She had an out-of-this-world sense of wisdom like no other at her age. So many of her peers honored and respected her opinion. As a strong leader and voice in her school, she was honored her senior year with the Southwestern Conference Leadership Award and had been chosen to sit on a committee at her Catholic school that decided the fate of those who had discipline issues. My daughter Koneisha experienced one of her greatest attacks when in Bridgeport, Connecticut, at the hands of the leader of Follies. My daughter devoted her entire high school years to help build an organization that failed her in every way imaginable. She was bringing so many of her friends into the organization and her self-esteem was at its highest. She even sold the most tickets out of all her peers, which helped packed the house. The founder of Follies deemed her a social and political threat because of her influence and vowed to take her down. It was relational aggression, which runs rampant in the political world, and she sought out to destroy my daughter, not knowing she was destroying her own organization. She had written a letter to her school claiming my daughter had dragged her across the stage and she feared for her safety. It just so happened her friends had witnessed exactly what had transpired. They had stated in their letter that my daughter had approached her asking to talk to her for a minute because she wanted to discuss the way she was bullying others and her. Verbal bullying, which can also be relational aggression bullying, was taking a toll on her. She was sabotaging her social standing. The witch hunt in Connecticut was overwhelming. This was something neither I nor my girls had experienced while in Michigan. I knew that the State of Connecticut was in a state of crisis. I knew my fight would be an uphill battle because not only were the adults bullies, but they were also leaders over the youth. This was God's purpose in my life. I have always fought against injustice, and the fruit doesn't fall far from the tree, but we all know bullying is a learned behavior, one I did not want my girls to pick up. Those who are bullied can become bullies. This has become a constant curse on the communities in Connecticut. It was hammer time. A time to take down. The Follies leader set up her own demise. It soon collapsed.

> *The curses of our people—Deuteronomy 28:32 (KJV): "Thy sons and thy daughters shall be given unto another people, and thine eyes shall look, and fail with longing for them all the day long; and there shall be no might in thine hand."*

Joseph's Coat Ministry (The Witch Hunt Continues)
Joseph's Coat was a place of many colors in Bridgeport, Connecticut. It was a church located on Noble Avenue formerly known as St. Paul's Lutheran Church before being changed to Joseph's Coat by Reverend Hevita. This church was named after the story of Joseph in the bible who his father Jacob blessed him with a coat of many colors. I was given the honor and privilege to work with a wonderful couple at a church called Joseph's Coat. They found favor in me and allowed me to lead their youth choir ministry. As I joined forces with Pastor Hevita and Joseph's Coat Ministries, I introduced him to a leader of Young Life in Bridgeport, where I was a counselor as well. It began to flourish. Jealousy began to flare from those who wanted power and control over the church. As soon as things were headed in the right direction, evil was lurking. The mission developer, Ms. J., became even more jealous of the collaboration between me, Pastor Hevita, and the Bridgeport Young Life leader. The green-eyed monster began working through these ladies, especially the main culprit, Ms. J. She and her imps (Satan's helpers) began making false allegations about the pastor to the head of the Lutheran Church in Chicago, claiming the pastor was doing drugs inside of his office. They

were deliberately spreading rumors, using one of the youth to spread the lies among the other youth. Ms. J. and other leaders joined forces in evil, and strange things began to occur. There were secret meetings; Ms. Max was booking events and getting paid without the pastor's knowledge, which caused chaos to the point where police were called to the church. These events were ungodly events that invited many different spirits into the atmosphere. Ms. Max even tried to place division between me and a cousin while trying to rent Joseph's Coat. These witches are real.

Can one witch lead many astray? Yes, one person can lead many astray and overtake a community in no time. They do it by manipulation, sowing seeds of discord, physical aggression, and bearing false witness. In one instance, the youth were eager to show up to a Bible study. This Jezebel spirit locked the door of the church so the youth could not go inside the facility. None of the youth left because the message was so powerful. We waited and waited and waited until the keys came from the pastor, and then that was one of the most powerful Bible discussions we ever had. The district office met with all of us regarding the false allegations about the pastor, but they had another agenda, which was to prevent our people from growing stronger in spirit; they released the pastor and stunted the growth of the ministry. As a result, the youth all scattered, and we lost most of them back to the streets. The more we use the hammer to build, the more the enemy's work is hard to dismantle.

At the end of the day and when we all were left scattered, after further investigation, the district office leader who believed the lie was fired, the mission director was fired, and the rest of her imps were asked to leave the ministry. Ms. J., the assistant to the bishop of the Lutheran Church in Chicago, went into early retirement and apologized to the Hevitas for being negatively influenced. These were the smaller evil forces the Most High had prepared me for because he would use me later for greater attacks. These scriptures played a role in my preparation:

Isaiah 5: 20–21 KJV: "Woe to those who call evil good and good evil, who put darkness for light and light for darkness, who put bitter for sweet and sweet for bitter!

Chapter 8

THE REBIRTH OF A CITY

In 2005, I was asked to be a radio personality for Gospel Alive Ministries. We began to collaborate with the City of Bridgeport's Health Department, which brought forth life to our city. There was free health screening, gospel music giveaways, free lunch, and much, much more. The community was at peace during this time, less violence, more unity. A "Day of Healing" was one of my first community events. This took place right after the health fair. Our collaboration with the Bridgeport community was a positive path to our destination. The Lord led me to call all those to the banquet who were poor, sick, lame, blind, and all gathered to hear a powerful message from our guest speaker, Pastor Shannon of Calvary Temple Church. At that time I worked for a regional network of programs, and the director at the time seemed like a just man and welcomed the faith-based organizations to help and the healing of God's people. All of God's children filled this place, the well, the sick, the mentally ill, and the challenged. They filled the Olivet Baptist Church in the evening, sharing their testimonies, local performances, free food and giveaways.

On this night a powerful testimony had manifested from one of my clients, Michael, who was notorious and was given to me as a joke because nobody wanted him. Michael was notorious for ripping stop signs from the cement and going from 0 - 10 just because. An extremely challenging behavior. But guess who had the last laugh? God moved through Michael in a mighty way. Before leaving this earth, Michael touched so many lives. You see, they knew how Michael was BC (before Christ) and could not believe how much he had changed after Christ chose him. He and I developed such a bond. Michael taught me how to love unconditionally.

One day, as he was sitting on the sidewalk of the house where I worked, he said that this glaring person looked over at him with a strong illumination around him; he described what he said was Christ. His description was not like we would imagine. This Caucasian man described Christ in a way we were not taught. He was so excited about seeing the Holy Spirit, and from that day on, Michael became a new person. This was a person who used to just yank the stop signs out of the cement because he couldn't have his way, telling everybody off; he was so angry, and it was not any fault of his own as he was just dealt a bad hand, being labeled at an early age, something that followed him up until his death. On the day of healing, Michael humbly testified about how Christ changed his life and how he no longer was filled with anger but instead filled with love and peace. This man had the biggest heart, and he truly loved me; we were so connected. A week before his death, I had a dream he was in an animated field of flowers with a huge smile on his face, proclaiming he had made it in paradise. One week later, the morning he died, I could not get out of bed; I couldn't move. In fact, it was the first day ever I called off work. I received a call from the supervisor stating Michael had died. When I saw Mike in the casket the day of the funeral, he looked like his soul was peaceful; an illuminated glow was around him. I was at peace; I knew he had made it in. It was truly a day of healing for all. When I think of Michael, I am so encouraged by this scripture: *2 Corinthians 5:17 (KJV): "Therefore if any man be in Christ, he is a new creature: old things are passed away; behold, all things are become new."*

Chapter 9

SECOND COMMUNITY EVENT: "NEW BEGINNING"

As we continued to build the wall using our hammer, the City of Bridgeport was in peace and love for a short time. We had it rocking with great gospel, promoting good health and unity. Fairfield University granted me my own radio station entitled *Taking Back Our Community Radio*. The WVOF 88.5 FM *Taking Back Our Community Radio* mission was to develop and grow bigger into other territories. This was our first event, held in downtown Bridgeport at the McLevy Green, where we brought in special guest artists, Isaiah D. Thomas and the Elements of Praise and Dr. Goldstone, who was everyone's favorite high school principal from Warren Harding High School, as well as my brother Keith DuBose and Sheena Graham Owens, who were honored for their years of commitment and excellence in the City of Bridgeport. At this time, I was too gullible to realize that the new mayor had a different agenda for our city, and I became a target of the new administration.

This new administration's team began taking every one down one by one, starting with the Director of Social Services, who had a mind to feed the community in the healthiest way, feeding them herbs, and giving them the free health care, which it needed. The Director had a belief in doing things in a natural way. As we built, the enemy continually tried to dismantle. The next person that was a target was the director of the recovery network of programs, who, as I have stated, loved collaborating with faith-based organizations. The city made it so difficult for him that he just walked away from his position. You see, when we don't share the same agendas, hell is around the corner.

The City of Bridgeport was gloomy by the day the new administration team brought in the gathering of the Vibes at Seaside Park, in which one of the featured groups was The Grateful Dead. That's when a lot of crimes began to happen. A lot of youth began to be murdered, along with a lot of other violence this particular year. The City of Bridgeport went from a place of peace into one of turmoil again.

Chapter 10

A FAMILY THAT PRAYS
TOGETHER, STAYS TOGETHER

While the Most High used me at different organizations, I had to tackle my very own family. One of my cousins was chosen as chairperson, and I was chosen as co-chair of our family. Our first year went the way it had been planned. It was a ministry-like environment with my brother Calvin, who was a DJ, held it down and kept the ministry going with great gospel music. Everything was so peaceful at Beardsley Park. We had so much love, praising the Lord, playing many games, with so much food and so much togetherness.

The following year more of our family attended the family reunions. We had our own shirts with a distinct color, and we knew who was related to whom by the color of our shirts. It was very organized, with games, popcorn machines, cotton candy machines, obstacle courses, horseshoes, etcetera. It was so beautiful, and then fear set in among our family. A rainstorm approached. My call was to pray away the rain and stay put at the park, which was a show of faith, but the final decision rested upon the reunion chairperson. They decided we needed to pack up and leave. As we were packing up and leaving, we were driven by families who stayed at the park and toughed it out. As we packed our things, driving past them, the sun suddenly came out, and it was sunny the rest of the day! This put a division in our family as we were driving past, seeing how faithfully the other families had stuck out the rain. This spoke volumes about our family, which had always been raised in ministry and taught by our grandparents, who had much faith; we realized we did not exercise any faith that day.

Either at the family reunion business or ministry, at our third annual and last reunion, I noticed that we were shying away from ministry in which our grandparents had sealed our lives. I can tell you that I share 50 percent of this blame. Yes, God took away my anointing due to my fall from grace. How could I reprimand anyone when I was walking in sin myself? I became hypocritical, and the family may or may not have known it, and that's where the loss of respect happened. At the same time, God had awakened me after this incident we had at one of our dance parties, Uniting Our Youth, but instead, the youth ended up almost going to blows. We prepared for a fundraiser for our family reunion. Allow me to set the stage before I go there. The reunion was advertised on Channel 12 News. Flyers were put up everywhere! The place was packed! Youth ages 18 and up to young adults and even the elders partake in this event, far from how our grandparents guided and raised us. The flyer advertised, BYOB! There was drinking, covetousness, provocative dancing which led to immature behavior, and intoxication which led to wrong decisions. Our grandparents were turning in their graves as to how we turned out. As tensions flared, I began to pay more attention and opened my eyes to the enemy taking over. At this point, I was powerless because this was judgement.

In families, the wisest approach is to allow the seasoned veterans guide our family and the youth continue to be under their guidance. It is quite dangerous to allow the youth to take over one's family as they are not seasoned. We gave permission for evil to roam that night seeking whom he could devour. We went from being a family that prays together to a family that preys upon one another. The night ended, and instead of us uniting our youth, the mission had failed tremendously because two cousins and their families almost went to blows over a woman with a big butt and a smile. Yes, this girl was poisonous! The place was in turmoil because somebody screamed, *"He's got a gun!"* Everyone started running out of the party earlier than expected. It was truly a disaster. When God has his hand on anyone and any family, we will be chastened much quicker than anyone else. I snapped back from the sin I committed and fell on my face before the Most High with repentance. I lost my anointing, and my gifts were on hold. As long as I kept my eyes on him and had my hands raised, I won every battle. But as soon as sin was allowed in and I defiled his temple, his hands were off me. Sin allowed the enemy into my home and family. If we knew our history, if the Hebrews kept their hands raised in praise, we won every battle without casualties. The minute we played the game of politics and business in the family, we lost whatever ministry that had been sown into our family. But because of grace, his mercies and the blood, the Most High is forgiving. I vowed to him I would never go down that road again.

The next year we were planning a Valentine's Day dinner dance. The Holy Spirit still spoke to me about connecting with people who are unequally yoked. While planning and organizing, I felt our family still hadn't learned our lesson and was taking a business approach and continued shying away from ministry.

As our family meetings went forward, I could sense a side eye as I would speak inside the meetings. I was no longer in sin and could see again. My guard was up, and my antennae were working again. And they had asked me about a facility at Joseph's Coat at which I had favor with the leadership. They wanted to know if they could use the facility. I agreed. A family member had warned me about their plans to serve alcohol in this church, and I had to take a stance. We were using this facility for the youth to bring us together, but the enemy had other plans. I refused to allow what happened the prior year to happen again, even if I lost relations. At this point we decided to part ways.

The hammer cannot be used to build Satan's kingdom again. This scripture comes to mind when I think about God's grace and mercy toward us: *1 Peter 5:8 (KJV): "Be sober and be vigilant because your adversary, the devil as a roaring lion, walks about seeking whom he may devour."*

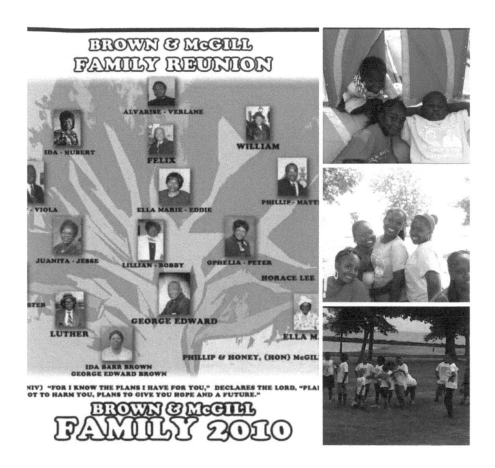

A Family That Preys Together

There is a huge crisis among our people of us preying on one another. Our roots were weakening and The Willie Lynch Theory is working as planned.

I am not here to enumerate your problems, I am here to introduce you to a method of solving them. In my bag here, I HAVE A FULL PROOF METHOD FOR CONTROLLING YOUR BLACK SLAVES. I guarantee every one of you that, if installed correctly, IT WILL CONTROL THE SLAVES FOR AT LEAST 300 HUNDREDS YEARS. My method is simple. Any member of your family or your overseer can use it.

I HAVE OUTLINED A NUMBER OF DIFFERENCES AMONG THE SLAVES; AND I TAKE THESE DIFFERENCES AND MAKE THEM BIGGER. I USE FEAR, DISTRUST AND ENVY FOR CONTROL PURPOSES. These methods have worked on my modest plantation in the West Indies and it will work throughout the South. Take this simple little list of differences and think about them.

READ MORE: HTTP://IMAGES.APP.GOO.GL/5TPLTBAPVC68QQWNO6

The churches are the number one contributor to our lack of unity in the community. The many churches with leaders who were called by man often covet true men and women of God and sought out to destroy the very same person The Most High sent to help. Also, the many differences created by different religions contributes to the division in our community.

Churches also have the obligation and duty to enhance the identity (spiritually) of the people so we can avoid identity crisis which plagues our community. Had we known our identity is hidden in the scriptures and we are the lost sheep who Christ came here for first, our pride, dignity, and respect will immediately be restored. It is because we as a nation do not know our history, our identity, and our culture, we began to shy away from our true God of Abraham, Isaac, and Jacob and started following other customs, which placed us in the bondage we are in today. You noticed almost each decade we switched cultures, from the blues, rock, to rhythm and blues, to soul, disco, and the longest-lasting, hip-hop culture, which seems to not be going anywhere, because WE ARE LOST! The Lost Sheep of Israel.

The Hip-Hop Culture is the longest-lasting culture, but it went from having some substance in the early 80's to utter oblivious which has our people and the masses ignorant shying away from the more meaningful things in life, like FAMILY (forget about me; I love you). The game changed in the early 90's when Satan totally took over the music industry. Money, power, and position have ruined our family structure. Sports came from Athens, Greece which fed our flesh more of the competitive and emulation nature all of which detours us away from our God given purpose which is to help others. Fraternity/Sorority (Greek) led us astray from our covenant relationship with The Most High through Christ. We began to follow Greek customs which are designed for us to not fulfill God's purpose over our life. Every day we wake up to fight 4 things which are Self (our thoughts, our image, esteem, etc), our flesh (fornication, adultery, lies, drunkenness, emulation, etc) the devil and this world's system which has taken over.

Because we as a nation did not know our history, our identity, and our culture, we began to shy away from our true God of Abraham, Issac, and Jacob and started following other customs, which placed us in the bondage we are in today. Each decade we switched cultures, from the blues, rock, to rhythm and blues, to soul, disco, and the longest-lasting, hip-hop culture, which seems to not be going anywhere.

Power and control have taken over our communities. One story about how family members would prey on each other like crabs in a barrel: A Connecticut Basketball AAU Program began, and my daughter Kiana was a rising, shining basketball star in the Bridgeport community. She was in training for quite some time with the trainer of Connecticut Impact. They worked well, and he introduced us to his team. Kiana's first year was a bust. But all the coaches saw her potential and found favor in her. As she began to further be developed, the following year my girl was one of the top players being talked about. She was dominating in all the pickup games to the point it was standing room only. It was time for tryouts. There were certain girls who had not made the team because their focus was more on the elite players. I convinced the founder of Connecticut Impact to allow me to coach the players who had been cut, creating a B team, which I added my daughter to. I decided to bring in my then-talented cousin as a coach so that our combining together could advance these girls to one day becoming top contenders. My cousin's agenda was quite different from mine—he wanted to take over as head. The founder of the program could sense my cousin would be a problem from the beginning since at a meeting he acted as though he were the head coach. I explained to the founder our sticking together as a unit only to get comments like "It is not us you should be concerned about," while looking at my cousin with a smirk on his face. Loving my family and not taking heed of the warnings, I proceeded with the season with him as my assistant.

These girls were special and talented but were not elite players yet. As time went on, our girls developed such an amazing relationship and started connecting almost immediately. I kept them praying together before every game, and they would congregate at one another's homes, which kept them closely connected. We lost our first game but began to bond with each other shortly after. Before long our record was 6–1. But as I kept them praying, others began to prey on our success, including my cousin, who loves power and control.

The Deception

The founder of Connecticut Impact approached me about concerns about my praying with the players. In my opinion, this was more about me getting in the way of his secret agenda, which others brought to my attention. This was about him building his program around his daughter. It made sense as I thought about it. He began to join forces with my cousin, who was there to assist me.

At this point he began to turn parents against me. He also began to call certain players to practice early without my knowledge. When asked why he was doing this without me knowing, he stated he had gotten permission from the founder of Connecticut Impact. I further explained to him that there cannot be two heads, and he turned into a beast at that moment. At that moment I decided to release him from his duties. He then took the girls he had brought into the program and left. A meeting was held with all parents, and it was stated to me that all the parents had voted to bring back my cousin. Most of the parents had no clue what was happening behind the scenes because I kept it quiet. He, the parent leader, and Coach B knew exactly what was happening because they each had their own agendas. The parent wanted her child to take over as lead, my cousin Coach B wanted full power and control, and the founder wanted his daughter in his program. Our team, which had developed quite a name so quickly, was shattering his dream.

I decided to remove myself, deciding this was a toxic situation and the leadership created a negative environment for not only with my team but also his entire AAU program. As I began to lose the parents, I began to lose the team members, who followed the wrong voices of the leadership who had developed relational aggression toward me.

As I wrote my letter of resignation, I was made aware of the fact that only a few parents wanted my cousin to lead the team. They were in the dark as to what was happening. They wrote to me individually, expressing their sadness. I did not want to give up on the girls, but because of leadership operating with such deceit, I had to protect the entire team from further divisiveness, undermining, and cutthroat behaviors. My cousin, the assistant coach, took over the team and they began to lose. The parents saw his coaching techniques and began to complain. The main parent who led the way began to fight with my cousin, resulting in a terrible rest of the season for young players who did not deserve the vicious acts of adults. There was an incident in the papers at their hosted event that tarnished their reputation, on top of the leader exposing himself. Immediately the entire program collapsed, and the youth were all scattered to different teams.

> *Blessed is the man that walketh not in the counsel of the un-godly, nor standeth in the way of sinners, nor sitteth in the seat of the scornful. Psalms 1:1 KJV:*

Money, power, fame, and control destroy a community. We had a strong, powerful culture that we lost. Our oppressors broke us down to the point of no return in this lifetime. Families today tend to not only fight for power and positions but oftentimes judge one another on their economic status—called classism—based on the kind of car one drives, the kind of house one lives in, where one works, lavish lifestyles, etcetera. For this reason, our children fall victim to such acts from adults, creating more of a mental health crisis. What happened to the ministry? What happened to forget about me; I love you (FAMILY). We need to stop acting like we are all that when we are nothing without Christ.

Walk in your purpose! Consider, a man approaches a farmer who is walking in his purpose, helping feed the population of this world, propositioning him with millions of dollars to destroy his own crops so he cannot feed the masses. Is this farmer walking in his purpose or thinking about his own self? He has sabotaged his own purpose in life. This is what families become, especially in our nation. What would we do for money, fame, position, power, and control?

> *Romans 16:17–18 (ESV): "I appeal to you, brothers, to watch out for those who cause divisions and create obstacles contrary to the doctrine that you have been taught; avoid them. For such persons do not serve our Lord Christ, but their own appetites, and by smooth talk and flattery they deceive the hearts of the naive."*

Chapter 11

REBUILD

Back to School Three-on-Three Basketball Tournament Sponsored by *Taking Back Our Community Radio* on WVOF 88.5 FM

 My vision in Connecticut came to pass. The agenda was to separate a community in Stratford by region and in the schools. I vowed to break that gap and build bridges for us to unite. The three-on-three basketball tournament was on its way to mending relationships. In fact, we were at our sixth annual back-to-school basketball tournament, and it was growing.

I wrote the vision on a sticky note after moving back home and stuck it on my computer to remind me of my daily short-term goals. The Bible states in Habakkuk 2:2 KJV And the Lord answered me, and said, Write the vision, and make it plain upon tables, that he may run that readeth it."

The three-on-three consists of half court play, three players to a team with one substitute, and the first to twenty-one points wins the game. This was so exciting and made the game so much fun and intense. Bridgeport had never had this before. Because I moved around so much, I was introduced to a lot of things to bring back home. Again, I began to build. Each year we showcased local talents, local DJs, and basketball players around the community that expanded across Connecticut. We had a special guest, three-time champion WNBA player Yolanda Moore, who motivated and encouraged the youth. The community came together with donations of free food and information, and we had several organizations donate various items to the youth. The champions had bragging rights for one year, receiving trophies and gift bags, etcetera.

After standing on his Word and after creating these huge events that attracted between five hundred and seven hundred youth in the community, the students went from fighting to building relationships and lasting memories. As a result, Frank Recchia of Channel 12 News featured me for the work I've done in the Stratford community bringing forth peace and unity among the youth. Word of advice: when you do things in secret, God will reward you openly. Keep the cameras away, for we as God's chosen people will become a target for trying to unite.

> *Deuteronomy 28:64–65: "And the Lord shall scatter thee among all people, from the one end of the earth even unto the other; and there thou shalt serve other gods, which neither thou nor thy fathers have known, even wood and stone. And among these nations shalt thou find no ease, neither shall the sole of thy foot have rest: but the Lord shall give thee there a trembling heart, and failing of eyes, and sorrow of mind."*

Chapter 12

SERVITUDE

For many years we have supported Habitat for Humanity of Coastal Fairfield County in many ways. My girls were involved in the Uniting Our Youth program and also played a part in the support, and in return Habitat for Humanity supported them whenever they asked. I can remember a time when they asked my girls to perform at the First Congregational Church in Fairfield with the gospel choir. My other daughter and I participated as singers as well. They raised thousands of dollars in excess of more than their goal because of my testimony and the powerful performance of my daughters. At that time, I had lost income and wasn't making as much money and fell behind on my mortgage. I shared my hardship with Habitat for Humanity. They acknowledged how wonderfully supportive my girls and I had been to them. They had raised so much money they were willing to help me catch up on my delinquent payments. The catch was they still brought me into the office to have me sign a new contract raising my mortgage two hundred dollars a month while creating payment arrangements that would allow me to catch up within one year. I finally got caught up on the mortgage. However, meanwhile, I met with a legal adviser who informed me that she didn't like how they were dealing with me in this situation. This really got me thinking about how my children and I were being exploited while they were gathering government grants, bank grants, sponsorships

from businesses, donations from the community, free material, and five hundred hours from the families of the homeowners as well as the homeowner. As I made conversations with different individuals on my street, I was hearing that the Hispanic families were receiving the much-needed help whenever they fell behind, but for us black families, they made it harder to catch up.

I began to calculate and ask questions. The house also had plumbing and leakage issues, which cost me more money to repair. The leakage caused mold throughout the home, which I had professionally tested. With all this, they had to either demonize me to get me out of the home or do it the right way and place our family inside another home until it was fixed. A lot of families faced this same ordeal. Some were helped, but others were not. Just as a note, I do not expect to live free, but what I do expect is for organizations to live up to their mission statement.

Do the Math

A substantial amount of money in the name of the Habitat homeowner was given to Habitat, along with public donations sponsored by GE. Westport National Bank granted me $8,000 with a five-year retention, all materials were free, and we used our hammer to build my home, volunteering over five hundred hours. Once all of this was done, the house was paid for before we moved in. At the time I worked, coached and volunteered, as well as worked my five hundred hours to make this dream come true, to become a homeowner. Mind you, while in Michigan, my husband and I almost earned six figures together but never became homeowners. For me this was a dream come true—at least I thought. It was more like a nightmare.

Families were so excited to get in this program in which they would do anything to just get the keys, including agreeing to have Habitat lawyers represent them in the closing, a huge mistake. We all were doomed from the beginning. The good part about it was that I was given the deed at the closing, which stated honestly the amount that they held and stated that Habitat for Humanity could never own or claim the rights or titles or demand interest. They and their successors were forever barred from the premises. I knew this would be valuable information for me soon. Most people weren't given the deeds, but I was one of the ones blessed with this information. My neighbor across the street became a target for helping me out. She was an African American single parent like me who also went through tough times but was not helped. Others and I wondered how the process worked and began to compare. This was after the information was disclosed that the Hispanics were getting help when they fell into hardship. A Hispanic neighbor had not paid rent in years, saved their money, and purchased a home. How were they able to get away with this? When I began to ask questions about how this process even worked and why they were asking families for their attorneys to represent us, that made me a target.

They began to confuse the payments on my account, claiming that I owed more than what I'd been paying, which was incorrect. My past due grew and grew because they wanted to collect all payments. That was when they placed my home in foreclosure. But because I continued to pay the taxes, they could not touch me. They held off the foreclosure until I was laid off from my job in 2013. It could not afford the taxes. In late 2013, after they realized that I hadn't paid the taxes, they began the foreclosure proceedings. During the proceedings it was claimed that I owed three mortgages. I obtained an attorney who was mystified at how I could hold three mortgages after my attorney had spoken with them. He tried to convince me to give up this case and that I would not win. Of course, I dropped the attorneys because I have faith. While I began to fight their attorneys myself, their attorneys' firm dropped out in the middle of the battle, and a more corrupt firm—with the same lawyer, because he jumped ship, who I will not name—picked up the case, and the judge ruled in their favor. I knew I had no chance, although the judge had my deed in his hands stating Habitat for Humanity was forever barred from the premises, including their successors. He still ruled in their favor, but I remember that this judge took me in his chambers before the case just to pick my brain to see how much I knew before the trial. He considered this off-the-record, but it helped the attorneys to see where my mind was. It was even on record that they forged documents because they didn't have the original documents that I signed at closing. The items that they showed me in the court I questioned, and I asked them if they had the originals. The judge intervened and said they did not need the originals. I knew that was not true.

The day of eviction, the Habitat for Humanity president and vice president came with the moving truck to eject me and my daughters out of the home, along with my grandbaby. They didn't follow proper protocol, and I asked them to get off my property. I knew that they weren't supposed to be there because they were forever barred from my property. I shared my eviction with the officers; the eviction was illegal, and there was no judge's signature on the eviction paper. They continued to try to intimidate me. Prior to this, I shared all my information with all city attorneys, state representatives, senators, and anyone who was a public official. They ignored my cries.

The Day of My Eviction

Several months down the line, I was served with eviction notices for the property I owned, including all rights, claims, demands, and interest. The only judgment they should have had was a judgment for me to pay them, not a judgment to remove us from the home we had built. They got even eviler, placing all my girls but my baby girl on this notice to be evicted. They wanted all of us to pay for me fighting for my people. The day came, and they were accompanied by the Stratford Police Department. As the police officer banged on the door, I refused to answer it. The Holy Spirit spoke to me to open the door. I believe he knew me and my girls would not have rested as if we stayed.

Stratford PD had it in for me because I had delivered a blow in exposing their racial practices, which made the *Washington Post*. Also, within their department, I exposed a veteran police officer who was helping the bad kids instead of protecting the innocent, causing him to go into early retirement and be glad to assist Habitat for Humanity. One of the black officers came into my home to help begin throwing my bags down the steps as if he were enjoying the moment, while the HFHFCC president stood in my home taking pictures. All had smirks on their faces as if they were proud to defeat me. The Spanish officer seemed very remorseful. As my children and I stood in their house and did not open the door, there was really nothing they could do because (1) the eviction notice was not signed by a judge and (2) my deed would have prevented Habitat for Humanity, the police officers, and the marshals from coming into my home. However, the Lord told me to leave and to keep my children protected because I wouldn't be able to live in peace if the Stratford Police had anything to do with it the rest of my time living in Stratford, so I used wisdom and just opened the door and peacefully left my home. All I could see were my daughters crying outside. I thank God my grandbaby was not home at the time. Even the dog was crying; it was truly a sad day. All the neighbors gathered around in tears to see what Habitat for Humanity had done to a family who had done nothing but support and give their all to this organization. This was enough to place fear in all the other homeowners.

I am here to tell you that not all Habitat for Humanity locations are the same. Rest assured, the one in Connecticut was built for servitude. It had become Habitat for Lawyers. Milliard Fuller's mission was "seeking to put God's love into action," and Habitat for Humanity's mantra was "bring people together to build homes, communities and hope" (https://fullercenter.org/millardfuller/). This mission failed our community and was an utter embarrassment. God had allowed me to go through this entire ordeal to expose the corruption of this organization and get the people the help they needed, especially the African Americans, who were not treated equally.

Not all Habitat for Humanity staff governed themselves in this manner. This is my story about the corruption in Connecticut. As a result, there were over three pages of foreclosures having to do with Habitat for Humanity lawyers being exposed for flipping homes. It went from sixty down to maybe only one or two families shortly after my encounter. Kim Lanham, who fought with me, is a veteran of the US Army, and because she was a witness to my situation, they also began to target her by placing her home in foreclosure. The judge never honored her payment, even though she had proof she paid, but still she *too* was evicted.

Ms. Lanham appealed the case. After the Most High prepared me to arrange her brief, her case was accepted in the court of appeals. Ms. Lanham gave sworn testimony in appellate court (https://casetext.com/case/ habitat-for-humanityof-coastal-fairfield-cnty-inc-v-lanham).

As a result, today homeowners through Habitat who are experiencing hardship can now seek assistance from Capital for Change! There is power in unity!

A new CEO sits at the head of HFHFFC, who sat on the Board at the time when all this transpired. If she wants to truly make a difference, it is not until they make their wrongs right, they would be able to move forward and folks gain back confidence in this once inspiring organization. If not, a dark cloud will forever be over their head.

> *Genesis 12:3 (KJV): "And I will bless them that bless thee and curse him that curseth thee: and in thee shall all families of the earth be blessed."*

CHRIS COOGAN AND THE GOOD NEWS GOSPEL CHOIR

With Special Guests:
'N His Image, Koneisha & Connie Johnson, and God's Chosen Ones

Sunday June 14, 5:00 PM
First Church Congregational
148 Beach Road, Fairfield, CT

Ticket Sales 203.543.1230

Suggested Donation $20 Adult • $15 Senior & Children

A portion of the proceeds will benefit **Habitat for Humanity** of Coastal Fairfield County

CONNIE KORNEISHA AND GOD'S CHOSEN ONES NAMES ON FLYERS AND EXPLOITED.

October 28, 2013

Via Email: flieto@lietoandgreenberg.com

40 Reef Road
Fairfield, CT 06824

Re: Habitat For Humanity v. Connie Johnson

Dear Frank:

I tried to contact you on Friday and appreciate your calling me back, but apparently we missed each other.

I would like for you and I to be able to look into this matter a little more closely. I was able to locate a copy of Connie Johnson's State of Connecticut Real Estate Conveyance Tax Return which shows that the full price of this sale was $█████ which is in accord with the allegations of the first two paragraphs of your complaint. I am mystified as to how there could be a second mortgage in almost the exact same amount. It seems to me that either it is someone else's mortgage and inadvertently Connie Johnson's name was typed on it or that it was executed and filed in error. I raise this issue because I have put the brakes on a contract which I was to have her execute when she brought your mortgage foreclosure papers to my office last week as I indicated to you in our prior call. Perhaps we can together talk to your client to see what's what because it is possible that we can still put this together, sell the property and get Ms. Johnson a few dollars to move to forward.

I also enclose a copy of a right of first refusal which Ms. Johnson forwarded to me which, if in fact there is only one mortgage, we would like to present with an executed contract.

I know that we are supposed to be in court next Monday on this, but in view of the above, perhaps we can get this resolved before then. I will be filing an appearance after we talk. I would appreciate your getting back to me.

Very truly yours,

/mh
Enclosures
bcc: Connie Johnson

53

017924   VI 2551 PG 048

QUIT CLAIM DEED

TO ALL PEOPLE TO WHOM THESE PRESENTS SHALL COME, GREETING

HABITAT FOR HUMANITY OF GREATER BRIDGEPORT, CONNECTICUT, INC., a non-profit corporation having an office and place of business at 1470 Barnum Avenue, Bridgeport, Connecticut, herein designated as the Releasor or Grantor, for the sum of ~~████████████████████████████████~~S, received to the full satisfaction of the Releasor from CONNIE L. JOHNSON, of ~~████████████~~, Connecticut 06615, herein designated as the Releasee or Grantee, does by these presents remise, release and forever Quit-Claim unto the said Releasee, his/her heirs and assigns forever, all the right, title, interest, claim and demand whatsoever as the Releasor has or ought to have in or to all that certain piece or parcel of land, together with the buildings and improvements thereon, situated in the Town of Stratford, County of Fairfield and State of Connecticut located at 56 Agressa Terrace, such premises being more particularly described on SCHEDULE "A" attached hereto and made a part hereof

TO HAVE AND TO HOLD the premises herein remised, released and quit-claimed with all the appurtenances unto the Releasee and his/her heirs and assigns forever, so that neither the Releasor nor the Releasor's successors or assigns, nor any other persons claiming under or through the Releasor, shall hereafter have any claim, right or title in or to the premises or any part thereof, but therefrom the Releasor and they are by these presents, forever barred and excluded.

The premises are hereby conveyed together with and subject to the terms, conditions, agreements, obligations, and easements contained in the Declaration of Easements and Restrictions and Party Wall Agreement by the Grantor dated December 16, 2003 and recorded in the Stratford Land Records at Volume 2326, Page 274 as it may be amended or supplemented. The Grantee(s), by acceptance of this deed, hereby expressly assume and agree to be bound by and to comply with all the terms, conditions, agreements, obligations and easements as set forth in said Declaration, as they may be amended or supplemented.

(In all references herein to any parties, persons, entities or corporations the use of any particular gender or the plural or singular number is intended to include the appropriate gender or number as the text of the within instrument may require.)

IN WITNESS WHEREOF, the Releasor has signed and sealed this instrument this 8th day of December, 2004

Witnessed by

[signature]
Barbara Ellis

[signature]

Habitat for Humanity of Greater Bridgeport, Connecticut, Inc.

By _[signature]_ Joan B. Mitchell.
Its Secretary

STATE OF CONNECTICUT   )
) ss. Bridgeport   December 8, 2004
COUNTY OF FAIRFIELD   )

The foregoing instrument was acknowledged before me this 8th day of December, 2004 by Joan B. Mitchell, Secretary of Habitat for Humanity of Greater Bridgeport, Connecticut, Inc., as her free act and deed and the free act and deed of Habitat for Humanity of Greater Bridgeport, Connecticut, Inc.

219.04
438.97

[signature]
Conveyance Tax Received
Patricia P. Abalowich
Patricia P. Abalowich, Town clerk
Town of Stratford

[signature]
Barbara Ellis
Commissioner of Superior Court

54

Chapter 13

THE WAR ON BRIDGEPORT

I had so many prophetic dreams, but I named the ones that were profound and stood out. In a prophetic dream, the Holy Spirit revealed to me a future event that would take place and end in disaster because the leadership had grown and allowed corruption. The dream showed that I was in a particular city pleading with adults who were leading our youth astray. They were drinking, partying, sexing, and all manner of evil filled this community. I didn't know exactly where this community was. While I was warning the masses, the sky became like an orange fire that began to form together. I began to cry out, screaming to all to follow me away from danger. Then branch brimstones of fire started falling from the sky. Only a few individuals followed me, and I ran to a place of safety—a place I called home in this dream—but when I looked back, the entire city blew up which means a cleansing will take place. After I woke up, I knew God was revealing to me a new assignment. It was being given in the city of Bridgeport. Satan's helpers had been bound for years, and he and his people were released from serving their term in prison. I made the mistake and voted him in 2005 into office in the City of Bridgeport. Dirty politics fooled many, including me. This was the last time I played the game of politics. Murders amongst the youth begin to rise again specifically on the East End vs North End. A city not built with Christ being the Chief Cornerstone will not stand.

Politricks was the same game that divided our people leading us scattered which brought our people into bondage starting in the 1600s and lasting into the 1900s.

> Deuteronomy 28-64: And the Lord shalll scatter thee among all people, from the one end of the earth even unto the other; and there thou shalt serve other gods, which neither thou nor thy fathers have known, even wood and stone. 65.And among these nations shalt thou find no ease, neither shall the sole of thy foot have rest: but the Lord shall give thee there a trembling heart, and failing of eyes, and sorrow of mind: 66. And thy life shall hang in doubt before thee; and thou shalt fear day and night, and shalt have none assurance of thy life: 67. In the morning thou shalt say, Would God it were even! and at even thou shalt say, Would God it were morning! for the fear of thine heart wherewith thou shalt fear, and for the sight of thine eyes which thou shalt see. 68, And the Lord shall bring thee into Egypt again with ships, by the way whereof I spake unto thee, Thou shalt see it no more again: and there ye shall be sold unto your enemies for bondmen and bond-women, and no man shall buy you.

One must remember, when God has chosen you to do a work and serve your purpose, he will bring you among your people to expose the enemy's tactics. Much like Moses was sent among his people to feel enough compassion to come back to help them, we must possess that same kind of energy today. Exodus 17:11 And it came to pass, when Moses held up his hand, that Israel prevailed; and when he let down his hand, Amalek prevailed. Nothing is new under the sun. As scripture cites: "Yea, though I walked through the Valley of the shadows of death, I will fear no evil!"

God had allowed me to go through this entire ordeal to expose the wickedness and corruption of variuos organizations, governmental, judicial, school and police systems. They are the greatest gang of them all teaching our youth their toxic ways. A video exposing the Connecticut Gang War was shown on YouTube but failed to expose the system which creates such an environment.

Ephesians 6:12–17 (KJV) reminds us:

For we do not wrestle against flesh and blood, but against principalities, against powers, against the rulers of the darkness of this age, against spiritual hosts of wickedness in the heavenly places. Therefore take up the whole armor of God, that you may be able to withstand in the evil day, and having done all, to stand. Stand therefore, having girded your waist with truth, having put on the breastplate of righteousness, and having shod your feet with the preparation of the gospel of peace; above all, taking the shield of faith with which, you will be able to quench all the fiery darts of the wicked one. And take the helmet of salvation, and the sword of the Spirit, which is the word of God; and having shod your feet with the preparation of the gospel of peace; above all, taking the shield of faith with which, you will be able to quench all the fiery darts of the wicked one. And take the helmet of salvation, and the sword of the Spirit, which is the word of God; praying always with all prayer and supplication in the Spirit, being watchful to this end with all perseverance and supplication for all the saints—and for me, that utterance may be given to me, that I may open my mouth boldly to make known the mystery of the gospel, for which I am an ambassador in chains; that in it I may speak boldly, as I ought to speak

Chapter 14

ENLARGE MY TERRITORY

 At the time there was an agenda to gentrify the community, including the rezoned places. The spirit of divination had begun. All three different projects: PT Barnum, Marina Village, and the Greens were sent to one school, called Bassick High School. All three had gangs and quite often fought and killed each other. They all now attended one school. I believe they were purposely combined so that these kids could kill each other off! But God had another plan in store for them. My plight continued for He uses the foolish things to confound the wise.

As God was using me to be a speaker at various schools, I ran into a wonderful principal, a woman of faith, who was a visionary and had great faith in what I was doing. She heard me speak at one of the functions and invited me to her Saturday Academy. While I was speaking with the youth, she absolutely loved my speech, and her vision was to create a girls group. This group of young girls who were leaders needed to channel their leadership in a more positive manner.

During the Dark times with gang violence 2013 -2014, I began to meet with these girls at first once every two weeks, and we developed the name of this girl group, "We Are S.E.T." S.E.T. is an acronym for Student Empowerment Team. This group had such a positive effect on this group of wonderful ladies; when we first met, they created a journal. My experience was relatable, and they heard me overcome those demons by the grace of the Most High. My setback was as a setup for his plan and purpose in my life. I gave them each a small book, and in this book, they had to record every day, and at the end of the night, who they hung out with, what they did, and what the outcome was. We would meet and discuss every two weeks what they did. This helped to open their eyes to which path they were going down. Before I gave them a book, many were on a road to destruction. I had them "enrolled to destiny," and they had to name all the things that required them to be on the right path to their role in life. To assist on their road to destiny, they were responsible for reading certain materials, volunteering their services, going to school, working, studying, and going to church. We reminded them that their road to destruction included drinking, drugging, partying, gossiping, and bullying, among other things. The entire concept really opened their eyes and made them more conscious about who they were around.

After that month of meeting with them, we had a retreat. This weekend retreat provided games, speakers, and free food, with icebreakers to start the sessions off. At the end of the night, we had "pillow talk," and some of the girls who were fighting one another or had participated in a lot of bickering ended up developing lasting relationships. We found out that most of them didn't even know why they didn't like each other, but it ended up being a most beautiful night as they began to bond.

Even more profound was that the next morning; we had some organizations come in and talk with them about the advantages of going to college and share with them their own personal experiences in college. A police officer came and shared a lot of things that he had experienced, and their eyes were opened further.

Once the weekend ended and they went back to school, they were happily bragging about their weekend. This group of girls continued with their bonding and eventually created a spirit team. This team was more like a "sisterhood" and a pep club. We assisted in the purchase of the banners, and we also purchased the cowbell and pom-poms. Not too long afterward, we designed and purchased We Are S.E.T. shirts for the pep rally. As soon as we successfully prepared them for their next walk in life, the enemy began to work. Note: Their "next chapter" we continued to build with the hammer!

Chapter 15
SANBALLAT & TOBIAH IN 2014-2015

As we continued to try and build the wall like Nehemiah had built the wall in Jerusalem, there was always going to be a Sanballat and Tobiah lurking around. A brief history of Nehemiah: Nehemiah and his builders, the Jews, vigorously hurried the work, while Sanballat and his associates organized their forces to fight against Jerusalem. Nehemiah prepared to meet the opposition and continued the work on the walls. Five different times Sanballat and his confederates challenged Nehemiah and the Jews to meet them for a parlay on the plain of Ono. Nehemiah was equal to the emergency and attended strictly to his work. Then Sanballat, with Jews in Jerusalem who were his confederates, attempted to entrap Nehemiah in the Temple, but the scheme failed. Sanballat's Jewish allies, however, kept Sanballat and Tobiah informed as to the progress of the work in Jerusalem. With the hand of the Lord upon Nehemiah, along with Nehemiah's farsighted policy and his shrewdness, he was kept out of the hands of these neighbor-foes.

The two assistant principals, Ms. B. and Mrs. Sliver, at Bassick High School were today's Sanballat and Tobiah. During this one pep rally that our S.E.T team had worked so hard to participate in, there were several issues. The whole school was really pepped up, and they had so much spirit, this one principal took it upon herself to force a quiet time for five minutes and we sat in utter silence in the gym. You know that this strategy killed the spirit. We Are S.E.T team and the whole entire gym were frustrated with the approach of this principal, and they read right past her as to what she was doing! This was the beginning of many sabotaging events against anything that I had to do with, including our S.E.T. team and the dance team. This principal, Mrs. Silver, Tobiah, had even purposely omitted the "We Are S.E.T." team from the yearbook, as well as my photo identifying me as the school's data analyst. She made sure we were not in history. Same game, different player. A complete sabotage, but I kept focus on the mission instead of the distraction.

Chapter 16

AS WE BUILT-WE KEPT FOCUS

The following year Mrs. M. was officially named the only head principal at Bassick High School. She was an African American woman who was strong as an ox. She had a strong presence about her. When she walked in the office, her presence demanded respect. Students had a level of healthy fear, knowing she didn't play around, and there were no holds barred. The reason why I stated she was the only principal was because the superintendent made all four principals the head leaders the previous year. Mrs. Smith was the overseer of them all. This brought about a lot of confusion, as you will see.

Mrs. M. came from the New Haven school district and out of retirement; in New Haven she was successful in turning around the school. She was faced with a fight of her life inside the wicked system where the blacks did not stick together. That is the City of Bridgeport. She was not prepared to face a new PTSO president who joined forces with the notorious School Board Maria. They both had the teachers' union, some board members, and the district's lieutenant on their side. The sabotage began. Mrs. M. didn't play and knew what she was facing. The dirty games of politics are not worth losing your peace and dignity over, especially when the parents do not fight.

This particular year, during Black History Month, Mrs. M. was out sick. Ms. B., the assistant principal, felt the need to try and sabotage the day. She would not allow some of the Black History Month Committee free from their other duties. One was a substitute teacher who was heading up my entertainment. Ms. Hump kept trying to contact her, but she refused to seek coverage for her. She decided to bring all the students down to the gym with her so she could fulfill her obligation.

This year was our second annual Grand Fair in memory of the late Garret Bynum, who passed away from diabetes. This Black History Month Grand Fair consists of a history fair, college fair, career fair, and health fair, all in the gym. In fact, the entire school was quiet the entire month leading up to the grand fair because they were learning things that were related to them. There were colleges, jobs, health care organizations, Army and National Guard recruiters present, and student projects were set up all around the gym. We had entertainment and performances by the dance team, WHHS band sharing their presence with us, poets, rappers, etcetera. The students worked extremely hard learning about their history. The entire community came together to celebrate and remember one of our fallen.

Ms. B., the other assistant principal in addition to Mrs. Sliver, had another agenda. Instead of trying to work hard with the students, she spent her time trying to tear it down. Ms. B. set out to get Ms. Humphrey fired from her position. Ms. B. and Mrs. Sliver were both later removed from Bassick High School. Mrs. M. served her purpose and decided to walk away as a result. The more we build as a community, the more the enemy finds ways to dismantle anything that is making progress for our people. Before Mrs. M. went back into retirement, Mrs. Smith requested to leave and eventually worked as principal at another school. They both did get to see the "We Are S.E.T." graduate. Mrs. Smith had the highest-achieving graduating class in decades. She did it the right way. No faking the books and no easy way for our students. She made them work hard! In the end they praised her during graduation. Mrs. Smith wouldn't have it any other way. Even though some were failing their sophomore year, they kept focused, pressed toward the mark, and have stayed together till this day. This was because of Mrs. Smith's vision and her believing in me to oversee some of her stronger leaders, who were a walking testimony to others.

NEWS

Bridgeport school arrests, suspensions down

Linda Conner Lambeck

Updated: July 5, 2015 12:13 a.m.

Credit to Principal Smith for bringing in outside organizations to help with the youth but the security department took credit in the article.

Mark 3:24 (KJV): And if a kingdom be divided against itself, that kingdom cannot stand.

During the 2014–2015 school year, our youth was faced with another blow. Not only did they try unleveling the playing field requiring that all students, only in Bridgeport, the youth had to make the CIAC's eligibility for fall sports is determined by the number of credits received toward graduation at the close of the previous school year, not the fourth marking period grades. You must have received credit in at least four Carnegie units of work for which you did not previously receive credit to be eligible for fall sports participation. This may include credits earned during the summer. Thereafter, marking period grades, not semester grades, are used to determine eligibility. You must take and earn passing grades in at least four of the quarter Carnegie units and meet the academic requirements of your school to achieve state eligibility. Along with me, a coach from WHHS, an assistant coach, and my cousin / chairperson of our family all fought for the youth. We demanded the hiring of more qualified teachers to challenge our students and to give them a curriculum that would spark their interest. Their attempt to stagnate our youth failed. Had they cared about our students, they would have held accountable the very people who had failed our students. If I wasn't challenged in my days and wasn't prepared to compete on a regional level, much less a district level, how prepared are our youth today?

They had to seek crafty counsel on how to destroy the youth with another tactic. The tactic was to divide Bridgeport public school athletics, which divided a community. United we stand; divided we fall. The enemy knows this. Why don't we?

The sabotaging continued in sports as they took WHHS and Bassick High School out of the most dominant leagues in Connecticut, only leaving Central High School in the hardest division, even though they were losing, to protect that side of town, which happened to be the more upscale. They set the precedent. This would not have happened in a suburban district, ever. This could not have happened without the approval of the board members at the time. Who sold us out? The board members were even with the blacks, who had a majority at that time.

I remember working in the office while the principal was on vacation. The assistant principal, Mrs. S., head coach of Bassick High School and the district athletic director, planned to hire the Bassick athletic director without the overseer principal's knowledge. They were playing the game of chess by lining up the pawns. They waited until Mrs. Smith was on vacation to make such a move. In came more corruption. They accomplished placing Harding High School and Bassick High School in a lower league. Oftentimes the boys' basketball team will play FCIAC teams and still dominate other sports such as football, volleyball, and track. Cross-country, girls' basketball, football, etcetera were headed by coaches who had losing records for years, which is unheard of at any other school district. Usually, if other schools in suburban communities have a losing record, you are removed from the position. At Kolbe Cathedral, if you had a losing record, you were gone because that was their bread and butter. However, in Bridgeport, Connecticut, the coaches who have losing records stay in their jobs for the longest time, all the while living outside the district. I believe this was a deliberate attack on the power to unlevel the playing field by leadership who has no stake in our community. Why is it that Central High School remains the only high school in Bridgeport District to stay in the FCIAC? Central High School just so happens to be in a more prominent district in Bridgeport. The suburban communities would never allow such a thing to transpire.

Chapter 17

YOU CAN'T WIN WITH POLITICS INSIDE THE SCHOOLS

Deuteronomy 28:50: A nation of fierce countenance, which shall not regard the person of the old, nor shew favour to the young:

As I was trying to keep the Word of God inside the schools after donating over thirty-three Bibles under Dr. Ramos's leadership, people from outside our district who worked inside Bridgeport public schools began to usher satanic books of sorcery and sex into the schools. The new principal in 2016–2017 was Dominican. He was a kind man who fell into the political arena and learned quickly he had chosen the wrong side of the track. I was his data analyst.

When he first arrived, he looked really kind, motivated, and energetic. As weeks went by, I saw his face change. His eyebrows were more arched and became like those of the others. I knew what that meant for me. He joined forces with the wrong team. He had me removed from the office, sending me packing to be under an assistant principal. I warned him that he was making a huge mistake and I would be praying for him and our school.

Even still after the move to the new office, I did not focus on the position; I focused on the mission. God had me there to do a job. The climate had changed. Hell was in the building, and the youth became rebellious and disrespectful because Mr. R. had canceled all after-school programs—well, certain after-school programs to the point the kids did not care. At this time a PTSO member had come up to me and the video game adviser claiming that there was a private meeting between the PTSO president, Mr. Benny, Lieutenant G. of the school district building and the principal with a plan to dismantle the after-school programs. What type of spirit would take away things the youth loved? How could this be? And what she had expressed to us happened exactly how she said it would.

Hell broke out in this school. There were fights on top of fights on top of fights, many office referrals, and suspensions. Expulsions were at an all-time high. The PTSO president, Mr. Benny was pleading with News 12 to stop exposing Bassick High School to protect the principal he had chosen for the position. That couldn't stop the media because the students posted on social media, making Bassick High School a laughingstock in Connecticut. There were many wonderful students inside Bassick, but if you take something they love away from them, they will rebel. The same scenario happened at Fisk University while W. E. B. DuBois's daughter and others fought against the very same form of oppression, taking away after-school activities.

Had history been taught to our students to prepare them for such attacks, the results would have been less turmoil and better organization.

> King James Version
> [48] Therefore shalt thou serve thine enemies which the LORD shall send against thee, in hunger, and in thirst, and in nakedness, and in want of all things: and he shall put a yoke of iron upon thy neck, until he have destroyed thee.
>
> [49] The LORD shall bring a nation against thee from far, from the end of the earth, as swift as the eagle flieth; a nation whose tongue thou shalt not understand;

[50] A nation of fierce countenance, which shall not regard the person of the old, nor shew favour to the young:

A Statement of Grievances against Fayette A. McKenzie as President of Fisk University

1. Students are allowed very little initiative or opinions of their own. They promise in writing to obey all present rules and "all rules that hereafter shall be made". They are admonished not simply to obey but to agree with the policies of the president and faculty or else to "get out of Fisk". The rules of behaviour are multitudinous and complex and many of them unwritten. There is no chance either by student council, by periodical, or by conference for the regular expression of student opinion and all student activities are not only supervised, but in most cases personally directed and checked by teachers.

2. The discipline which supports this situation is again and again, unjust and unreasonable. Students are continually threatened with dismissal from the university, with or without charges and with the attendant disgrace. A student has been placed on probation for conducting, with the permission of the president, an exercise to honor former Professor Work, and then ordered not to reveal the fact of his probation on pain of further punishment. A student has been dismissed because he signed a petition against compulsory study hour for college students. A girl has been dismissed peremptorily for stealing and when her innocence was proven, no apology or public statement was ever made. Repeatedly students who have been sent away with or without charges, have had great difficulty in securing from the institution, authoritative statements of their class standing. This discipline is supported by a wide-spread system of spying and tale-bearing. The chief of the faculty spies is a professor who heads the department of biology, who has never had a full college course or a college degree, and who left the

2

public schools of Bowling Green because the colored community did not regard him as fit to teach. The distrust of students on the part of the faculty, the distrust of the faculty on the part of the students, the disposition of the president to libel and accuse the whole Negro race, the atmosphere of fear and suspicion, the factions and discontent among both teachers and students, are but reflections of the failure of President McKenzie as an executive.

3. The teaching force is not satisfactory. The president arrogates to himself all power and there is no real consultation with the faculty. Most important decisions are arrived at by secret conference. Colored teachers are gradually being forced out and no well-trained successors appointed. Immature white undergraduates are repeatedly brought in as teachers and Southern white persons are being gradually put into positions of authority, - persons whose attitude toward the Negro race is not satisfactory. The yearly change in the personnel of the teaching body and the number of students who do not remain to finish their courses both indicate a serious condition.

4. There is deception in the actions of the president. The academic standard claimed by Fisk is not justified by its present work. The college enrollment as stated in the catalogue is not a statement of the truth. The college department both in administration and discipline, is submerged by the lower departments. In order that no criticism may be made upon the actions of the president, teachers are required to make promises that amount to engagements not to tell the truth. Students are similarly coerced by threats and there is reason to believe that sometimes mail has been tampered with. There are continued instances of petty tyranny and a determination to force persons of strong individuality and leadership, either among teachers or students, out of the institution.

5. President McKenzie is making every effort to increase the

The dance team was fighting hard to reestablish the after-school program. They attended SGC meetings, sharing their thoughts on how dance teams had helped them grow and kept them busy. They still ignored the cries of the students. So I had a private meeting with Dr. R., and I informed him that I knew about their private meeting. This reminds me of this Bible scripture Psalm 83:3–5 (KJV): "They have taken crafty counsel against thy people and consulted against thy hidden ones. They have said, Come, and let us cut them off from being a nation; that the name of Israel may be no more in remembrance. For they have consulted together with one consent: they are confederate against thee."

He stated that was not his decision, it was Lieutenant G.'s decision. The same individual taking credit the prior year for his security team turning around Bassick HS (please see photo). I informed him, "At the end of the day, It was your decision. The bottom line is you were the principal and the head." He agreed, and he reinstated the dance team and all the after-school activities programs. Relationships are either connected to your destiny or your destruction. Properly Placed People Prevent Problems and add value to your life. Improperly placed people devalue your life which can be destructive. This one person was the counterfeit. We began preparing for the black history celebration, and peace was restored throughout the building. The students started practicing getting ready for the black history activities, and it became a joyous occasion. It was an all-day event held inside the gym that included a career fair, health fair, history fair, and college fair. Music, food, entertainment, and games were all a part of the festivities. We had even invited the original Freedom's Rider to Bassick HS. No incidents were reported. The place was full of joy, laughter, peace, and togetherness.

This was the first time this year that Dr. R. had witnessed such work from the Lord. Dr. R. was so pleased with how the youth had behaved on this day, and it brought forth unity and relationships again. The rest of the year was peace and love. A sense of calmness came upon us all, and Dr. R. and I became very close. In fact, I was the first person he confided in that he was resigning. Dr. R. made his wrongs right. At the end of the year, Dr. R. truly praised my efforts and focus. I've grown to really respect him for all that he has done by bringing the youth together. I even put aside my differences with the PTSO president to keep the peace. A wise man will make mistakes right. As far as the dance team, they continued to be together for another year.

The next season they worked hard raising money to compete in the nationals during my last year at Bassick before the powers that be broke up the union. They went on to take seventh place in all-around and third place in their division. Had they stayed together, they would have eventually made it all the way to the top.

Proverbs 29:12: "If a ruler listens to lies, all his officials become wicked."

AFTER THE RESTORATION OF AFTER-SCHOOL ACTIVITIES,
JOY WAS BACK IN THE COMMUNITY!

Chapter 18

THE PLOT THICKENS

 A new principal, the first black male to hold the position, in 2017–2018, did not sit well with the PTSO president. Relational aggression reemerged because he had his focus on a Caucasian assistant principal from Harding High School. He made it a point to sabotage Dr. Williams and tried to get me to join forces with him. I refused to join forces with the PTSO president, which placed me as a target. The union president of NAGE (National Association of Government) propositioned me with the same. Ephesians 5:11 And have no fellowship with the unfruitful works of darkness, but rather reprove them. They must not have known me. The leader of the Black History Month Committee sabotaging my own belief in the advancements of our people? In fact, it was later learned that the PTSO president feared I would run for his position. In an email I've obtained, Mr. Benny reached out to a retired teachers' former union president, asking her, If I ran for a position on School Governance Council, would it be a conflict of interest?" She directed the question to Senior Staff Attorney, Connecticut Association of Board of Education (Documentation at the end of chapter). The Attorney's explanation was, "I understand the concern that some may have. But the idea is to have parents' participation as parents." Wait, shouldn't our interests be the same—what is best for our children? This was clearly another agenda in this sick quest, and I had no such interest.

Mr. Benny, the PTSO president, had no knowledge of my knowing about his sick motives in having me and Dr. Williams both removed from Bassick High School. Mr. Benny began to team up with a one-time enemy, a racist teachers' former union president from Bassick, Mr. Costello had gotten away with directing a racial slur to a student and brainwashing students to turn against me. (Documents shown at the end of chapter). Mr. Costello also went on social media (Facebook) slandering me and Dr. William's name claiming we had relationships. Mr. Benny also went on social media slandering my name claiming I took monies away from the student. Went to the extreme of helping our enemy.

Mr. Benny was not understanding the agenda set forth in Exodus 1:9-10 has happened in Egypt, has happened again today.

Exodus 1:9-10

[9] And he said unto his people, Behold, the people of the children of Israel are more and mightier than we:

[10] Come on, let us deal wisely with them; lest they multiply, and it come to pass, that, when there falleth out any war, they join also unto our enemies, and fight against us, and so get them up out of the land.

Our oppressors were so afraid our people would join forces with the Hispanic community, they had to act quickly to demonize myself and Dr. William's name and reputation so we could not be influences. Bottom line jealousy and ignorance but I forgave. This book is about exposing wickedness and principalities in high places.

The assistant principal, Ms. B., who sabotaged the Black History Month event, covered for this racist teacher during Dr. R.'s reign in the 2017 school year. As a result, he sought to take me down. Dr. Williams had no chance of succeeding at Bassick High School. It was a set up to get him out by not providing any support. Remember me sharing with you that Mr. Benny pleaded with News 12 about reporting fights during

Mr. R.'s reign? He began to search for negative things among our youth, sharing it on his Facebook page to make Dr. Williams look bad. Wasn't this a total contradiction? Dr. Williams's demise was set up before he walked through the door because he was up against demons destined to remove him from the beginning. He didn't fit their agenda. His true, bold, and no-nonsense approach, which was like that of Joe Clark, threatened the very essence of their being. He cared too much about the youth, and the teachers weren't having it.

Dr. Williams, an Alpha Male who immediately called pecking orders without fear was about to straighten out the athletic department, the teachers who had slacked, and the PTSO president. This type of male intimidates the powers that be, and they will try to minimize their stature by limiting resources, lack of cooperation or demonization. He was holding all accountable—those who showed up late daily, those who did not take their jobs seriously, and those who were not educating our youth. He was holding all accountable—those who showed up late daily, those who did not take their jobs seriously, and those who were not educating our youth. He had a masterful plan for a strong pathway for the youth, but this did not fit the agenda of gentrification taking place in all the inner cities throughout America. As registration began to increase at Bassick High School because there was a sense of pride, dignity, and respect among our students, demonizing also began because of too much power in one school. Anyone who helped the youth in the right way had to be dispelled or disposed of.

The Athletic Department During Dr. Williams's Reign

I allowed my baby girl, who was an honor student and known basketball player, to attend Bassick High School during the 2016–2017 school year because I had faith and belief that the school would rise. My daughter and her team were a very talented group of girls. The first season could have been better if the team hadn't been so confused. Once she and another one of her teammates who played on the athletics AAU team joined forces at Bassick, they, along with twin sisters, led the team to their first playoffs in thirty years!

I had begun inquiring about parents coming together to support our youth. When students see the support of their parents and we are on one accord, the excitement brings a different level of school spirit and pride. I also asked the girls' cheerleaders squad to cheer for the girls as well. It was like pulling teeth, but it eventually happened.

I had such high expectations for these girls. So much talent on one team. But I knew the head coach dilemma needed to be addressed this year or it would be a season doomed from the beginning. The athletic director and all the coaches fought me against this truth. He had another agenda for our youth and parents. Divide and conquer. At the time the head coach acted as the assistant coach and the assistant coach acted as the head coach. This often confused the girls' basketball team, as well as the referees. I discussed this with them to no avail. I asked when they would be having a parent meeting since there had not been one the past year. I had questions about explicit music during the games which was setting lower moral standards in our education system. They had no intention of parents coming together supporting our youth and setting better standards. In Fact, it has been years since a parent meeting had been held at Bassick High School; as a requirement according to CIAC rules and regulations a parent meeting must be conducted. The teachers who held students accountable for doing the right things were not following the rules and regulations of the league. This really bothered me because I wanted what was best for this entire team.

As they finally called a so-called parent meeting, I was the only parent invited to the meeting. Me, Dr. Williams, the principal, and another community leader showed up for this meeting. I was hoping we would be in accord trying to bring parents together and do what was right by our youth. It is so sad that our people are willing to sell out our babies for power, money, and control. My thinking is to always come together and unite people. Our oppressor's job is to divide and conquer, the oldest trick in history, and we are still asleep. A story that could have ended up a story of triumph and victory if our men had risen and protected the men and women in our community. I loathed the fact that our black men could not see the wrong in this siding with our oppressors. Our coaches and the athletic director had another agenda. Things must be done in decency, and in order to win and do what is right by our youth. We needed an established leader first and foremost! If the head is not right, the body is not operable. The athletic director disagreed with what I was saying about the head- ship because, of course, he had a different agenda. As the season went on, we took one of the most talented players from Curiale Middle School. My daughter and she played together and were well coached at Capital Prep by a great coach named Coach Craig Davis. He held a parent meeting and had wonderful things lined up for his girls. This is what really inspired me to share what he did with Bassick's girls.

Even with all this talent, I knew they wouldn't win because of leadership's way of thinking. Parental support and unity play a huge part in the victory of our youth. The girls eventually made it to the semifinals, along with the boys' basketball team. They had proven that our girls and our boys in the urban communities could measure up to anyone if given the right opportunity by leveling the playing field. Had the coaching staff been in the right alignment, I believe that the girls' team would have made it all the way. Remember, God cannot bless any mess.

As far as my daughter went, she fell out of love with the game because of the adults and politics. Much like Kyrie Irving & Kwame Brown, because they did not play the system's game, they will exclude and try breaking down a strong man taking away one's confidence, much like they did Kiana, no fault of her own. Not because of what she did but because her mom saw right through the agenda and was trying to bring together our people. Despite all the controversies, Kiana did attend D-2 Basketball at University of Bridgeport.

The demonization began with rumors that Dr. Williams and I were having a relationship, which was total gossip. The teachers' union president spread this rumor on social media. He made it a point to bring down every black person in office at Bassick High School. Human Resources did nothing to protect us and continued to allow this to go forth. The attacks picked up after the successful Black History Month celebration, which was an hour and a half production entitled *Many Rivers to Cross* by our Black History Month committee and Build ON. Our students were learning who they are as a nation that had been scattered across the world because of our disobedience. They were learning that they are the chosen people of God who are now the lost sheep. They were learning the way before 1619—our truth, our story, uncut! Yes, we had to go!

How does the lion pride overturns the King of the Kingdom? It's called a Turf War, when lions join together to wage war against the king lion in a bonded coalition to overthrow and take over the Pride. That is the nature of the beast.

The plot got thicker. The PTSO President began to attack Dr. Williams on social media when I started putting up photos of our Black History Month celebration, claiming Dr. Williams was a racist. He joined forces with Teachers Union President to form the coalition to bring down the Lion King of Bassick.

He even began to tag every board member and city officials on my post, and they did not hold him accountable. This has become the norm for the PTSO president, who has now been voted in as a board member under Mayor Ganim's team. A complaint was filed with CHRO, and in sharing this complaint, they did not allow me to speak about this in my hearing. This is how deeply corrupt the system is; it is set out to destroy the people of the Most High. Our people are so focused on our own economic well-being, we are continuing to sell out our community to maintain the false sense of wealth. We must wake up. Despite all the attacks, enrollment increased by close to three hundred students, office referrals were down, and students had a sense of pride, dignity, and respect. Bassick was rocking and on a move. Mission accomplished with the dismantle of the District PAC & breaking up the Lion's True Pride. A spiritual "Black Wall Street!" But we shall return with great power and glory in His name and build again. We were first, now we are last ......last shall be first.

From: Johnson, Connie
Sent: Wednesday, November 15, 2017 11:36 AM
To: Costello, Chris
Subject: Inappropriate Statements

GM Mr. Costello,

A few students, one being my nephew in which it was his second day in your class, approached me about a negative comment you made regarding me at the end of the day which is extremely unprofessional and lacked judgement. My Nephew felt he had to defend his Aunt in your class which had created a negative environment. Why should this be Mr. Costello? This is a first impression you left with him. Myself and his parent had asked for his class to be removed at this time. This is the second incident that I know of you were involved in that was cruel and unethical. One being a racist comment to a middle eastern student last year in which you did apologize and now about your fellow co-worker in front of other students. A teacher plays an important role in the structure of our students in this community. You (Teachers) are also a huge influence and one might ask the question, are you apart of the problem here at Bassick especially as Union Rep? Lastly, every moment is a teachable moment and what you have taught these students is not best for our community.

Concerned Co-Worker/Parent,

Connie Johnson
Data Analyst

https://mail.aol.com/webmail/en/en-us/PrintMessage   4/

From: Costello, Chris
Sent: Wednesday, November 15, 2017 12:38 PM
To: Johnson, Connie
Subject: Re: Inappropriate Statements

Good Afternoon Ms. Connie,

First, let me start off with an apology. At the end of the day , EVERY day, my 7th period, which happens to be my best behaved period, is interrupted by announcements. I can never close a lesson and when you are a teacher, closure of a lesson is imperative to gain insight as to what was hard in the class and I was going to go over the answers to the test they were taking. I did make the comment that the announcements took too long and that the reading of them seemed to take forever. I am sorry your nephew, which I did not know was in that class at that time was upset. I did find out he was your nephew as he told me after, that it was his Aunt doing the announcements. I noticed he is failing all 4 classes that are on his schedule. Perhaps I am not the only teacher he finds troubling? Perhaps interventions should be put in place for him to succeed if he will no longer be in my class. I care about all my students and for many many years have been told by the students themselves that I am their favorite teacher.

Again, we have never had a problem with each other Ms. Connie, and until now we have treated one another with great respect. I appreciate all that you do for this school and the time you put into it.

However, with all due respect, this email is truly what is unprofessional. You could have come to me directly-but instead-you chose to have a closed door meeting with several of my students without their parents being present and without me having any knowledge of such actions with an administrator. The students told me today that they did NOT come to you as you say, but were told to come to an office by a security guard, where they were interrogated-many of which said they felt very uncomfortable in the situation. Also, I find it very rude and unethical that you bring up a situation from last year that was found to be resolved and Dr. Ramirez said that in 28 years, he had not seen a teacher behave in such a professional and outstanding matter after I made the mistake. The one true mistake I have made in 10 years in this profession. That student and I have seen one another since and everything is fine. I have even been asked to write her a recommendation.....

Please do not tell me what role a teacher plays, as I have been one and a very good one at that for 11 years, having an outstanding rapport with my students and impeccable evaluations over that time period. I think we both know what and who is the problem here at Bassick and I promise you, if you gave a survey to the staff it would NOT be myself. There is a faction that is happening in this building over the last several years that many of us teachers are aware of, but cannot speak of, because we are afraid of the repercussions. If you need to speak on this matter further you can contact Gary Peluchette and we will sit down and discuss it. I would like it to end here. I have no reason to believe it won't. Again, I apologize for this matter, but I feel as though it has been blown out of proportion and I am being targeted, because I am the only union representative in the building that represents the large majority.

Thank you for your time.
Chris Costello
Bassick High School

MR. COSTELLO TEAMED UP WITH MR. BENNY TO HELP THE
AGENDA TO RID THOSE HELPING GOD'S PEOPLE.

LIFT
every
VOICE
celebrate BLACK HISTORY MONTH

"Our School District...News YOU Can Use!"

Volume 5 Issue 6   February 2018

BASSICK'S GOT TALENT!

Special Point of Interest

- Dates to Remember
- Parent Engagement TIPS
- Principals Matter!
- February School Menus!

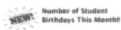 **NEW!** Number of Student Birthdays This Month!!

Inside this issue:

PRESIDENT'S DAY

Bassick Dance Crew (BDC) are a group of talented young dancers which has been together for 3 years and generating noise around town. They have been featured at various events such as MLK I have a Dream, Bridgeport's BOE Meeting and other shows which sparked standing ovation and thousands of views on Social Media. BDC is on it's way to the Nationals April 20 - 22 of 2018 in hopes of winning 1st place.

The Choir performances includes City Hall, Bridgeport Board of Education, MLK "I have a Dream" and ConnectUS at the Klein.

Drama Club performance at MLK "I Have A Dream."

Bassick Dance
team made it
to The
Nationals

BASSICK HIGH

Newsletter   Feb.—March 2018

Congratulations to all the New National Honor Society Members. The Inductee Ceremony lead by Mrs. Varghese was such a well organized program we will never forget. Also, thanks to all who helped organize such an elegant evening here at Bassick High School. The standard has definitely been set.

Congratulations to the Boys & Girls' Basketball Team qualifying for the States as well as them ranked in the top 10 in states for the first time in several decades. Also, the Bassick girls being ranked in the top 50 in the states out of 700 HS teams. The Lion's Den is the place to be!

We would like to thank the Art Dept. for accompanying our students on a Fairfield University Trip to the Art Museum to study the painting & drawing from the Artist "Richard Lyle."

Congratulations to Coach Blank with a successful Football Sport's Banquet.

The Drama Club, Choir and Dance Team all had excellent performances at the "I Have a Dream" program at the Klein Memorial. Also, all three were featured in this month's district calendar.

Dr. Williams is glad to report a successful mid-term evaluation. Keep up the great work Lions.

Also, congratulations to one of our outstanding vocalist, Reyes Huerta, who wowed the audience with his Frank Sinatra's voice at the BOE meeting this past month. He's also competing Nationally.

Itzel Sanchez & Topacio Reyes, Mrs. Walsh's Students, took 3rd place in the District Science Fair. The name of their project was entitled "Human Brain Testing Musical Brain." Congrats to you all!

Last but not least, congratulations to Anastee Durham for an invite to attend the National Leadership Forum at Yale University for Academic Excellence in the Field of Business.

QUOTE OF THE DAY

Others can stop you TEMPORARILY but you are the only who can do it PERMANENTLY.
~Zig Ziglar~

02/05/2018—Bldg. Committee Meeting in Bassick's Library 5:30 pm—7pm

02/06/2018—Bookfair at Barnes & Noble 5:30—6:30pm

02/08/2018—Winter Season Senior Night for Girls

02/22/2018 Anti-Bullying 5:30pm—7pm

02/24/2018—Best Cheer Competition for Cheerleaders

02/25/2018—Winter Season Senior Night for Boys

02/28/2018—Black History Month Production 10am & 1pm

Afterschool Activities

- Astronomy Room 359 Mon. @ 2:30 pm—4:30 pm
- Bassick Dance Crew Thur. & Fri. 3:30pm Auditorium
- Build On Thur. Room 163 2:30—3:30pm
- Chess Club Room 301 Tues. @ 2:30pm
- Choir Room 246 Wed. @ 2:30pm
- Christian Club Room 205 Thurs. @ 2:30pm
- Drama Club Tue. & Thurs. @ 2:30 Auditorium & Room 246
- Video Game Club Room 241 Tue. & Thur.
- Jazz Band Room 246 Fri. 2:30
- Student Council—Mon. Room 241
- Robotics---Wed. @ 2:30pm

DR. BYRON WILLIAMS, 2017-2018

Any parent with a child enrolled in the school is eligible for membership on the school governance council. The law is broad to allow for as much participation by parents as possible. I understand the concern that some may have. But, the idea is to have parents participate as parents. The issue may be that she does not feel free to express her opinions since she works for the principal. That is a different potential problem. But if there is an open seat and you have a candidate who would be an active participant who wants to make a difference for students, then it sounds like a great opportunity to me.

I am including Dolores Mason on this response. She is the go to person in Bridgeport for school governance council issues.

If you would like me to do a school governance council workshop or training, let me know.

Shouldn't we all work cohesively?

Best,
Rebecca

Rebecca E. Adams, Esq.
Senior Staff Attorney
Connecticut Association of Boards of Education
81 Wolcott Hill Road
Wethersfield, CT 06109-1242
(860) 571-7446

CABE: Dedicated to strengthening public education through advocacy, education and service to boards of education.
[Like us on FB 3]<http://www.facebook.com/ConnecticutAssociationBoardsEducation>
And Join Our Community

From: Corliss Ucci
Sent: Monday, May 21, 2018 9:19 AM
To: Rebecca Adams <radams@cabe.org<mailto:radams@cabe.org>>
Subject: FW: Schools Governance Councils

From: Edna Garcia <State128@aol.com<mailto:State128@aol.com>>
Sent: Monday, May 21, 2018 8:58 AM
To: Corliss Ucci <cucci@cabe.org<mailto:cucci@cabe.org>>
Subject: Schools Governance Councils

Good Morning
I have been asked by the PTSO President at Bassick High School, Mr. Albert Benejan, to help him find a response about a situation: We know that the SGC requires to have on its board 5 teachers, 7 parents and two students, the question we are asking is: Can the school secretary who is staff, and has a daughter at Bassick serve as one of the parents? The controversy that aroused from this was that she was staff, therefor would not be impartial as she is the Principals secretary.
Thank You for any assistance you can provide. Please respond in writing as we need to show your response to those interested in this matter.
State128@aol.com<mailto:State128@aol.com>
(203)727-0444

Last email on this page shows motive of PTSO President of Bassick HS (Encouraged to read all!!)

I WAS THE ONLY SECRETARY WHO HAD A DAUGHTER ATTENDING SAME SCHOOL AT BASSICK. PTSO TRUE MOTIVES & POLITICAL GOALS. HE NOW SITS ON THE SCHOOL BOARD

Chapter 19

BACK HOME

As my brother and WHHS Alumni Kcith, Alumni Katrina, Alumni Alexis, and I closed arguments regarding changing the name of WHHS to another name. Our arguments successfully convinced the Board Members to keep the name as we pointed out the constant destroying of history, especially black history, and the importance of keeping the name of WHHS for this very reason. Other alumni were not so much committed to the fight in this effort. Moreso, the ten percenters.

The Talented Tenth, (1903), concept espoused by black educator and author W.E.B. DuBois, emphasizing the necessity for higher education to develop the leadership capacity among the most able **10 percent of black Americans. Today's 10 % have become more like Beta Males**. Many are used to help our oppressors gentrify urban communities. Reason being, they are willing to sale out their people to maintain their lifestyles. Mainly all in Political Office in Bridgeport are considered Beta Males. Once they get before their true bosses in the community, the ones who have taken crafty counsel against our people, the Beta Males take a seat.

Do you remember my third prophecy? Moving back to my alma mater was quite challenging. Well, I thought this was truly the end of my prophecy. It's not my timing, but the Most High's. This was a chess move on their part. This principal is used to doing their dirty work. He is known for putting out his very own people so they can't prove discrimination. There is always one willing to sell out his people for the love of money and power. He was headstrong about getting me out of the district. It started one day with him taking away my job duties, although I was under a contract. He placed me under one of his assistant principals, all of whom were manipulated by Mrs. Sliver. Yes, you remember Sanballat? She was the assistant principal at Bassick who tried killing the spirit at the pep rally. She was removed from Bassick and placed at WHHS, my alma mater. This was a perfect storm. Mr. Brown, the principal, the 10th percenter, couldn't wait to target me. His character was like a Beta Male, nice face to face but an email gangster, which I will explain soon. He appears macho but often faces problems or confrontation passive aggressively. He also draws his power from witches and warlock type of people to make him appear as an Alpha Beta. In other words, An Ahab in scriptures. Men like these, our oppressors love to move them on top.

He began on the first day of school, accusing me of going over to Bassick High School during school hours.

He must have felt embarrassed after I informed him that I used my lunch break to withdraw my daughter from Bassick. I then asked him about the policy for lunch breaks and how we used them. Of course, he did not respond. The rest of the harassment and targeting went as follows:

1. Mr. Brown accused me of trying to petition a dance group two weeks later, which was false. One of my dancers from Bassick saw me and was so excited, she went to asked Mr. B. if she could begin a dance group. Of course, that was not a part of his agenda. This man is taking up space on this earth.

2. Mr. Brown accused me of letting in an WHHS alumnus after school, when in fact he was inside the building and had the nerve to write me an email. He saw me walking with the alumni after school and questioned who he was. The alumni were let in the building by another staff member.

3. Mr. Brown reprimanded me in an email about a diagnostic given incorrectly to the EMS based on the symptoms of a student who could not breathe and was rushed to the hospital. Later he learned I contacted the main office to contact EMS, and they shared what they were the ones who shared the information. Again, he had the nerve to place everything in writing, not knowing it would one day be used against him. Instead of congratulating me on my quick response, he just could not help himself. The curse of bullying runs deep among leaders in the community and leads to the path of destruction in our community. Our youth deserve better! The very image God created, which was supposed to cover the women in our community, was used to abuse his power to bring down his own people for power, control, and the love of money, who was just trying to be of help to the very community that raised her to be a leader? The type of leadership in existence today is a learned behavior and is harming our youth, turning them into manipulative bullies, something running rampant in Connecticut.

Mr. Cocoran played an important part to fulfill the agenda of total control over Finance and Data. I was the last Data Analyst they needed to get rid of, and this was how they did it. They changed my duties from Financial Secretary (Data Analyst) to Data Support Specialist (Manage School's Data). A perfect plan to confuse. After given perfect 5 for several years on my job performance, I was rated a 1 (poor performance) in a job I never did before.

Mr. Corcoran begin to so call punish me by further humiliating my daughter. Allow me to share other bullying tactics used against my daughter by. He invited me and my daughter to an award ceremony because he was her admin. He claimed my daughter would be receiving lots of awards. Well, he never called my daughter for the awards; in fact, the librarian later gave me the award in the summertime, after she had graduated.

As for my daughter's basketball coach at WHHS, she decided to play her out of position most of the season, even though she was one of her best players. An intelligent coach would have known she played at her best as a forward. Kiana was quick on jab, faking, mid-range shot or attacking the basket from the wing. The only coach who understood her game was her AAU Coach from the Brooklyn Stars, Head Coach Phree. The unlearned coaches played her as a point or shooting guard. The WHHS coach played ,y daughter as a power forward and sometimes a Center position. In my opinion, this was done out of spite.

One of the biggest games of her season was against Kolbe Cathedral High School, and college coaches attended. The head coach decided to bench my daughter until there were three minutes remaining in the fourth quarter. She then decided to approach her, kicking her in the foot to get her attention. She then nodded her head for her to go inside the game. My daughter is the mildest-mannered individual you would ever want to meet. The look on her face was one of anguish and sorrow. She did not move off the bench. The coach must have felt bad for her actions and decided to give a loving speech at senior night about Kiana. Kiana handled herself with such poise and respect. I told her, "Kiana, let the Lord handle all these dark forces!" The whole entire audience witnessed this happen, and it was the talk of town. I told my daughter, "You keep your head up!" The coach was later struck in the head with a softball, leaving her out for a while from teaching and coaching with head injuries. My daughter later went on to play Division 2 Ball at a University. She further realized while in college, she felt she was moving further away from the Lord with indoctrination and that her personal dreams must be set aside to pursue her purpose. You see, when you are purposed led, you will be in the pit for a season but in due seasons, will end up in the palace as Joseph. We can't abort the purpose which is planned later to provide a harvest for God's people during the season of Famine.

As for Mrs. Sliver, who secretly rules WHHS as she stands clear like Jezebel. Oh yeah, the Ahabs who sniff behind her (the lead and assistant principals) and do her dirty work as she makes sure her name remains clean. How conniving one woman can be who surrounds herself with men. She was masterful at removing many of the black strong leaders from WHHS so, she could remain on top. She played the game of chess extremely well. Mrs. Sliver cleaved to a Caucasian parent by the name of Ms. Tracie at WHHS to groom her into being the next PTSO President in a predominately minority high school. She and Mr. Brown (Ahab) forcibly moved aside Mrs. Davis, who happened to be Black as the PTSO president. This was apart of the gentrification process. Mrs. Davis had no means to spend the PTSO monies for children and teachers while I wasn't given the privilege to do my Job as Financial Secretary in which I have always made sure the children and teachers were always supplied with much. Again, we did not fit their Agenda of gentrification.

Despite what was going on, I must say the students at WHHS were woke. They are extremely bright leaders which are hard to break. During the year they showered me with gifts and kind words even though I didn't do half as much for them as I did at Bassick. Even though this principal was trying to shut me down any which way he could, it didn't stop me from giving encouraging words, advice, and love to these students at a moment which was needed in their lives. At the beginning of my second year at WHHS, I chose to take my peace of mind back by stepping out on faith. Once I took my peace back and resigned from my position by stepping out on faith, I was able to pursuit my God given purpose by becoming an author and serving others in His way instead of the Worldly System way. Peace and freedom mean everything! We must take back our life before taking back anything else.

We all must flee Babylon. We have got to get out of her and not partake in her sins. If you don't flee from Babylon, we will be destroyed in Babylon. Do not be deceived thinking you can defeat this powerful spiritual force. Christ even had sense to flee his own hometown he had no honor in. I decided to shake the dust off my feet and count against them the day of destruction. During this ordeal I had no representation from my union because they were in cahoots with the City of Bridgeport to dismantle and take control of the budget and data. I made a request for grievance; he did not file one on my behalf. They had been working alongside them to push forward with their agenda, to get rid of the data analyst and the data support specialist, and those two positions boil down to this fact: they who control the data and budget control the masses. I warned the Nage President that the city will use him and spit him out. And it came to pass! They repaid the Nage President by taking away his security guards' outfits which looked like police uniforms and having them dress like the students. Yes, the security team dresses in khaki pants and Izod/Cherokee/Dickies/Barco shirts. God doesn't like ugly and all who follow will suffer.

As for the city council and half the board members, they ushered the new superintendent right into his job, with no experience leading any school, no possession of a 093 certification at the time and still had not obtained it; never worked as a teacher but rather as a counselor. This says a lot about the direction in which our City of Bridgeport is going. They were involved in trying to demonize and destroy the reputation of Baltimore's deputy superintendent, who had applied for the position in Bridgeport. He was already prepared and had a wealth of experience with the Department of Education and the urban community, as a superintendent holding an 093 Certification, a principal holding an 092, and a teacher. Dr. Brice expressed his concerns about the youth and the dirty politics in Bridgeport. He expressed his concerns about the tactics of a city council member and community member setting him up to meet with a board member he did not know and had not met at a previous interview. Ms. B., Sanballat, was promoted to having her own school in Bridgeport, Connecticut. These are the very same people who claim they have the best interest of their own people in mind. They are building a city without the Most High and again choosing evil over good. This is the crafty council planning against us in every urban community throughout the United States. The plan is to depopulate us. They must first empower another nation to go up against us while they sit back and watch. They used the Hispanic community leaders to do the dirty work in Bridgeport.

Isaiah 5:20 (NKJV): "Woe to those who call evil good, and good evil; Who put darkness for light, and light for darkness; Who put bitter for sweet, and sweet for bitter!"

In 2 Esdras 6:9 (KJV Apocrypha), we read: *For Esau is the end of the world, and Jacob is the beginning of it that followed.*

This is a system without the Most High that is destined to take out anyone and everyone who opposes them if God allows. Remember, all power is in his hands, and no weapons formed against thee shall prosper.

I felt the need to write this in my book, which is more powerful than any court case. I am back home in a town that captured my heart when I was younger. The Bible states, "Though I have afflicted you, I will afflict you no longer" (Ps. 83 (KJV)). They have said, "Come, and let us cut them off from being a nation; that the name of Israel may be no more in remembrance."

WHEN HARDING WAS OLD, THEY HAD BETTER SPIRITS OPERATING OUT OF *LOVE!*

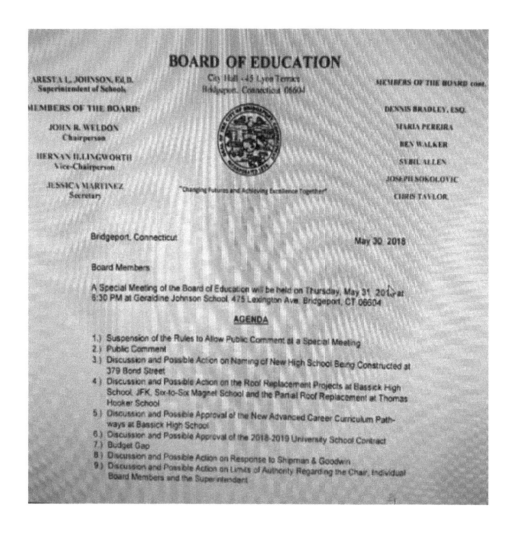

BOARD OF EDUCATION

ARESTA L. JOHNSON, Ed.D.
Superintendent of Schools

City Hall - 45 Lyon Terrace
Bridgeport, Connecticut 06604

MEMBERS OF THE BOARD cont.

MEMBERS OF THE BOARD:

JOHN R. WELDON
Chairperson

HERNAN ILLINGWORTH
Vice-Chairperson

JESSICA MARTINEZ
Secretary

DENNIS BRADLEY, ESQ.

MARIA PEREIRA

BEN WALKER

SYBIL ALLEN

JOSEPH SOKOLOVIC

CHRIS TAYLOR

"Changing Futures and Achieving Excellence Together"

Bridgeport, Connecticut

May 30, 2018

Board Members

A Special Meeting of the Board of Education will be held on Thursday, May 31, 2018 at 6:30 PM at Geraldine Johnson School, 475 Lexington Ave, Bridgeport, CT 06604

AGENDA

1.) Suspension of the Rules to Allow Public Comment at a Special Meeting
2.) Public Comment
3.) Discussion and Possible Action on Naming of New High School Being Constructed at 379 Bond Street
4.) Discussion and Possible Action on the Roof Replacement Projects at Bassick High School, JFK, Six-to-Six Magnet School and the Partial Roof Replacement at Thomas Hooker School
5.) Discussion and Possible Approval of the New Advanced Career Curriculum Pathways at Bassick High School
6.) Discussion and Possible Approval of the 2018-2019 University School Contract
7.) Budget Gap
8.) Discussion and Possible Action on Response to Shipman & Goodwin
9.) Discussion and Possible Action on Limits of Authority Regarding the Chair, Individual Board Members and the Superintendent

AGENDA (3) GENTRIFICATION - TRYING TO DESTROY THE HISTORY OF WHHS AND ALL IT'S ALUMNI ATTEMPTING TO WIPE OUT OUR GOD'S PEOPLE.

AGENDA (5) – DR. WILLIAMS BROUGHT FORTH A NEW CURRICULUM NOW BEING USED TO THIS DAY AT BASSICK HS BEFORE THEY DEMOTED HIM.

Chapter 20

AND WE'LL RISE UP

Once you begin to make strides in a community, building up things, our oppressors cannot stand our unity and will find ways to dismantle it, just like Black Wall Street in 1921. The story read: In 1921, Tulsa, Oklahoma's Greenwood District, known as Black Wall Street, was one of the most prosperous. African American communities in the United States. But on May 31 of that year, the *Tulsa Tribune* reported that a black man, Dick Rowland, attempted to rape a white woman, Sarah Page. Whites in the area refused to wait for the investigative process to play out, sparking two days of unprecedented racial violence. Thirty-five city blocks went up in flames, 300 people died, and 800 were injured." It went on to read, "'Nine thousand people became homeless,' Josie Pickens writes in *Ebony*. This 'modern, majestic, sophisticated, and unapologetically black' community boasted of 'banks, hotels, cafés, clothiers, movie theaters, and contemporary homes.' Not to mention luxuries, such as 'indoor plumbing and a remarkable school system that superiorly educated black children.' Undoubtedly, less fortunate white neighbors resented their upper-class lifestyle. As a result of a jealous desire 'to put progressive, high-achieving African-Americans in their place,' a wave of domestic white terrorism caused black dispossession. Defense of white female virtue was the expressed motivation for the collective racial violence" (https://daily.jstor.org/the-devastation-of-black-wall-street/).

As I learned while I was going through this whole ordeal with the public school system, you must know, lawyers have connections bringing on attacks from every which way to keep the people of God confused. I kept the fight for our people by introducing what is now House Bill 5124 which had been passed in March of 2020: An Act Requiring Landlords to Notify Tenants of Foreclosure Proceedings. This bill will help prospective tenants not be taken advantage of by greedy landlords taking your money and not paying the mortgage. In most cases they will not conduct repairs, living amid unjust enrichment.

Matthew 11:12 (KJV): "And from the days of John the Baptist until now the kingdom of heaven suffereth violence, and the violent take it by force.

Official Summary/Bill Text   Comments

Tweets   Similar Bills

Official Summary/Bill Text

Joe Gresko State Representative 121 District supports -
on behalf of Connie Johnson a
constituent she wishes to prevent families from facing
hardship like the ordeal she endured.
This bill would require full disclosure to a prospective
tenant by a landlord of a pending
foreclosure on the property being rented. Connecticut's
Tenant Bill of Rights would be
improved if it included disclosing foreclosure
proceedings on a property being rented.
Transparency in a rental agreement is paramount and
that should include tenants being
notified of pending foreclosure on the property they will

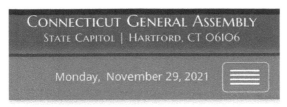

Raised H.B. No. 5124
Session Year 2020

AN ACT REQUIRING LANDLORDS TO NOTIFY TENANTS OF FORECLOSURE PROCEEDINGS.

To require landlords to notify prospective and current tenants of foreclosure proceedings and to permit tenants to seek court appointment of a receiver upon receiving such notice.

Introduced by:

Housing Committee

$\mathcal{P}$ BILLS

BILL PRESENTED BY CONNIE JOHNSON EXPOSING CORRUPTION IN THE JUDICIAL SYSTEM AND BIAS TO LANDLORDS IN THEIR WRONG.

The reason for this bill was because another corrupt landlord which is all over CT lost his home a month after me moving in. Auction sign was placed upon property, and he never fixed the weightier repairs in the home. The courts have indeed helped again on this matter tampering with evidence. I appealed this matter and had damaging powerful proof. They removed an entire Docket from off the court system. I sent proof and complaint to the Judicial Committee in Hartford.

I will encourage you to check the CT Court case Docket # 2018-BPH-CV5002800-S, Appellant Court #SC 20219 and AC 44952 cases with evidence completely vanished.

The Most High uses us to expose darkness in high places but how can He use you unless he brings you to it? Unjust Judges and Rulers will be judged right before our eyes. I applaud the character and integrity in the Just Judge in the Ahmaud Arbery's case. Proverbs 29:2, When the righteous are in authority, the people rejoice; when the wicked beareth rule, the people mourn.

Ephesians 6:12

King James Version[12] For we wrestle not against flesh and blood, but against principalities, against powers, against the rulers of the darkness of this world, against spiritual wickedness in high places. For I feel like apostle Paul and Malcom X at times. Paul stated. " Thrice was I beaten with rods, once was I stoned, thrice I suffered shipwreck, a night and a day I have been in the deep;

In journeyings often, in perils of waters, in perils of robbers, in perils by mine own countrymen, in perils by the heathen, in perils in the city, in perils in the wilderness, in perils in the sea, in perils among false brethren." I know, when we walk in faith, your purpose and proclaiming The Lord as our savior, will protect us. No weapon that is formed against thee shall prosper; and every tongue that shall rise against thee in judgment thou shalt condemn. This is the heritage of the servants of the LORD, and their righteousness is of me, saith the LORD.

My people, I know they have been stealing your property through the Water Company, tampering with evidence in the court system, but God will repay us double for our trouble. Especially those they Mark as troublemakers.

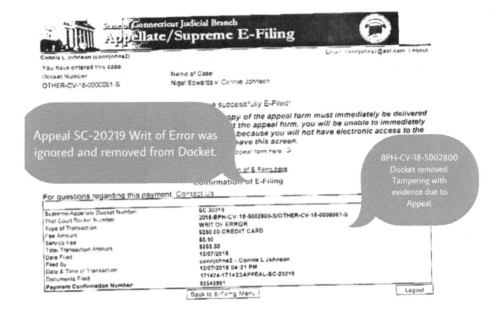

Deuteronomy 30:3 King James Version: 3. That then the Lord thy God will turn thy captivity, and have compassion upon thee, and will return and gather thee from all the nations, whither the Lord thy God hath scattered thee.

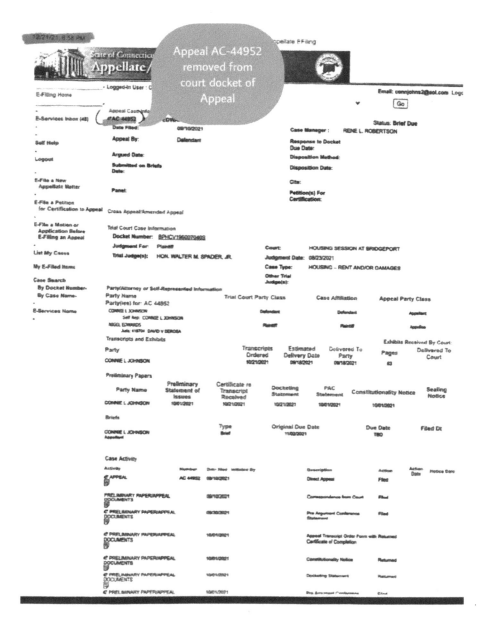

THE COURT OF APPEAL SENT IT BACK TO SUPERIOR COURT. MANY LOST
PROPERTIES DUE TO TAMPERING WITH EVIDENCE, THIS IS THE NEW WAY
OF BLACK WALL STREET SINCE INTERROGATION. THEY ARE USING THE
JUDICIAL SYSTEM TO DISMANTLE INSTEAD OF DROPPING A BOMB.

THIS IS DIRECT PROOF THE SYSTEM IS NOT JUST AND GOES AGAINST THE PEOPLE OF GOD. IN THIS PHOTO, YOU WILL SEE CASE # 44952 UPLOADED DOCUMENTATION BUT NOT FILED.

MOTION FOR EXTENSION	AC 2230053 07/08/2022 NIGEL EDWARDS	Appellee Brief Extension Date:07/11/2022	Granted	07/14/2022 07/14/2022
BRIEF	07/11/2022 DAVID V DEROSA	Electronic Version of Brief		
BRIEF	08/05/2022 CONNIE L JOHNSON	Electronic Version of Brief	Rejected	
MOTION FOR EXTENSION	AC 2230224 08/11/2022 CONNIE L JOHNSON	Cross Appellee/Appellant Reply Brief Extension Date:	Returned	08/11/2022 08/11/2022
PRELIMINARY PAPER/APPEAL DOCUMENTS	08/31/2022	Assignment Form (Response to Docket)	Filed	
PRELIMINARY PAPER/APPEAL DOCUMENTS	09/16/2022	Assignment Form (Response to Docket)	Filed	
DISPOSITION	Court	Opinion	Disposed	10/18/2022
PRELIMINARY PAPER/APPEAL DOCUMENTS	10/18/2022	Rescript	Filed	

APPELLANT CASE DISPOSED SIGNED BY CHIEF JUDGE.

Chapter 21

HELP IS ON THE WAY

"My people, I am here to tell you, help is on the way." God will come back and redeem his people first. He said, "First shall be last, and last shall be first." Who could this be he is talking about? He has also stated, in Revelation 2:9, "I know thy works, and tribulation, and poverty, (but thou art rich) and I know the blasphemy of them which say they are Jews, and are not, but are the synagogue of Satan." Think about which nation of people suffered the most throughout the centuries. He is coming to redeem us from our oppressors. Yes, America is the second Egypt we will exodus from. A system built on slavery, Pegan worship, capitalism and idolatry.

Here is a prophecy about us in the beginning of the book. Genesis 15:13-14 (KJV):

> [13]And he said unto Abram, Know of a surety that thy seed shall be a stranger in a land that is not theirs, and shall serve them; and they shall afflict them four hundred years;

> And also that nation, whom they shall serve, will I judge: and afterward shall they come out with great substance.

[14]And also that nation, whom they shall serve, will I judge: and afterward shall they come out with great substance. As well as

Deuteronomy 28:68 KJV

[68]And the LORD shall bring thee into Egypt *again* with ships, by the way whereof I spake unto thee, Thou shalt see it no more again: and there ye shall be sold unto your enemies for bondmen and bondwomen, and no man shall buy you.

1619 – 2019 ends 400 years "AGAIN" after which, tribulation will be upon the land as we are in now.
Servitude.....Judgement....Exodus.....Promise Land (Parallel to Genesis 15)!!

Revelation 18:4

"And I heard another voice from heaven, saying, Come out of her, my people, that ye be not partakers of her sins, and that ye receive not of her plagues."

I will encourage you to read our history in Deuteronomy. No other nation fits this prophecy more than our people.

It will be a great multitude, but it can be you if you can just believe in accordance with Acts 16:31(KJV): And they said, believe in the Lord Jesus Christ, and thou shalt be saved, and thy house. That if thou shalt confess with thy mouth the Lord Jesus, and shalt believe in thine heart that God hath raised him from the dead, thou shalt be saved. For with the heart man believeth unto righteousness; and with the mouth confession is made unto salvation. Romans 10:9-10(KJV) It doesn't matter what color you are the scriptures states that every nation, from all tribes and peoples and languages will stand before the Throne and the Lamb in Revelations 7:9, which means we must be justified by faith. The Lord is coming with thousands upon thousands of his holy ones (His Elect) to TAKE BACK this world, and it's its entire community. If we follow his lead, take up the cross, and follow Christ, we can use the hammer to build our communities, one person at a time. First shall be last and last shall be first.

> *Thus, saith the Lord; Though they be quiet, and likewise many, yet thus shall they be cut down, when he shall pass through. Though I have afflicted thee, I will afflict thee no more. Nahum 1:12 (KJV)*

This is *good news!*

ABOUT THE AUTHOR

Connie Johnson a mother of 4 and grandmother of 6 is a shining example of the resilience and awesome power of the human spirit. She was born in Bridgeport and graduated from Harding High School, Connie furthered her education at Dorsey Business School, Connie navigated her way through the business world for several years while married and raising a family. The year In 1999, Connie found her Lord and Savior, Jesus Christ, and while pregnant with her last child, Connie spent the entire 9 months basking in the presence of the Lord by reading the word of God. It was then when that a personal relationship was formed between her and the Lord. By a cruel twist of fate, the Lord led her back home to Bridgeport, CT, and through her faith, her purpose in life had been revealed. God gave her the Holy boldness to go in and possess the land. I Connie was instructed to spread the Gospel and take back what the enemy has stole from our community. The only way for Connie to take back the community was to first Take Back her own possessions. To take back something, first means it was stolen. Connie knew she would face strong opposition but was willing to leave all to follow Christ. Tremendous She faced opposition from church members, family, and the community of those who did not know Christ. But through endurance and long-suffering, God had begun to restore her home, family, and health with new relationships with Godly brothers & sisters in CHRIST. Connie began working for Challenging Behavioral Adults at the Regional Network of Programs.

Currently, Connie has settled down and is enjoying life while residing in Virginia as an Author and Entrepreneur.

TBOC Sponsors: as followed: City of Bridgeport City Wide Health Fair; City of Bridgeport's Senior City-Wide Health Fair; Sickle Cell of Association Disease of America Walk A-Thon; Annual Prayer Tabernacle Health Fair. TBOC received honors from the following organizations: 2005 received recognition for outstanding support to the Liberian Community by LCAC (Liberian Community Association of Connecticut), 2008 Holla Back Community Service Award from

Jerry Green Gospel & WNHU 88.7FM, 2008 Honoree Al Aziz of Bridgeport for Hard work and Dedication to the Bridgeport

Community, Diamonds In The Rough, 2010 Honoree, 2009 Honoree Black Pride of Bridgeport, Ct., Honorarium Chair for the 2011 Sickle Cell Of Disease Association of America Walk-A-Thon raising thousands of dollars, Citation from the City of Bridgeport, General Assembly and Senator Richard Blumenthal: 2011 recipient of Women of Year from Juneteenth of Fairfield County and recognized by Lyle Jones of Save Our Babies for motivational speakers at State Prisons as well as Women of the year Jineteenth, Bpt, CT.

CONTACT US TODAY!

"Remember, it's not about how you fall, but about how you finish!"

Email
Takingbackourcommunity@gmail.com

Facebook
https://www.facebook.com/takingbackourcommunity

Instagram
www.instragram.com/connie.johnson.1800

Twitter
Connie.Johnson@J28929962

Phone
Tel: (203) 543-9047

CPSIA information can be obtained
at www.ICGtesting.com
Printed in the USA
JSHW071101120223
37572JS00006B/81

9 781685 155629